21ST CENTURY HOUSE

21ST CENTURY HOUSE

JONATHAN BELL

LAURENCE KING PUBLISHING

LAURENCE KING

Published in 2006 by Laurence King Publishing Ltd
71 Great Russell Street
London WC1B 3BP
United Kingdom
Tel: + 44 20 7430 8850
Fax: + 44 20 7430 8880
e-mail: enquiries@laurenceking.co.uk
www.laurenceking.co.uk

Text © 2006 Jonathan Bell

This book was designed and produced by Laurence King Publishing Ltd, London

A catalogue record for this book is available from the British Library

ISBN-13: 978 1 85669 453 7
ISBN-10: 1 85669 453 4

Designed by Hoop Design

Printed in Singapore

Cover: Natural Ellipse, Tokyo, Japan, 2002. Endoh Design House and MIAS
Frontispiece: House on the Alentejo Coast, Portugal, 2003. Aires Mateus e Associados

Just a few years into the new century, creating a definitive picture of the twenty-first-century house is a far from practical proposal. The centennial (and millennial) desire for novelty traditionally invests a nascent era with a set of defining characteristics, signposts that point the way forward, mindful of the way we have come. In this accelerated age, grand movements in art, architecture and design have been reduced to fashions and trends, their transience and impermanence an indication of our impatience to label, qualify and classify, and then move on.

In architecture, as with all elements of culture, it seems inconceivable that a new era should be without its own definable ethos. Yet even in the early years of the new century, it is not easy to pin down exactly what constitutes the emerging residential architecture. Of all architectural genres and genuses, the house is perhaps the most enduring symbol of change and innovation, a neat, self-contained statement of intent that, when analysed en masse, should reveal essential truths about aesthetics, social dynamics and, that concept crucial to architecture's key obsession, modernity. Few could deny that there are several key themes running through contemporary residential architecture, themes that reflect the plurality of contemporary taste, and the social and political status of the house.

Rather than set out to define a visionary manifesto, *21st Century House* is an attempt to locate these themes, to trace their evolution and where they are going, and to identify which, if any, are most deserving of our attention. The book also demonstrates how architecture is increasingly related to the wider cultural sphere and how the image of the 'modern house' has evolved – and devolved – and considers the

introduction

[1] DU PLESSIS HOUSE, Paraty, Rio de Janeiro, Brazil, 2003. Marcio Kogan Architect

[2] LEVITTOWN, Pennsylvania, USA, 1952–

sources of the technological and aesthetic developments that shape and reshape residential architecture with dizzying frequency.

Throughout the twentieth century, the single family private house was fetishized as the epitome of modern architectural achievement, an object desired by many yet achieved by few. In terms of Modernist propaganda, the house played a pivotal role, both as a means of architectural expression and experimentation and as a testbed for new forms, new materials and new spatial arrangements. For better or for worse, the single family home became an iconic device, a stylistic and ideological calling card. For young architects, the 'first house' was the defining project, the crystallization of their intent and the wellspring of their creativity. Does this attitude still prevail? Has aesthetic and stylistic pluralism done away with the dogma and the sheer, typology-challenging novelty of the modern house? Or has the avant-garde been thoroughly subsumed into the mainstream? Are there emergent forms and methods poised to take its place?

More than 80 years after the first buds of the Modern Movement burst forth, contemporary architecture has lost much of its crusading zeal, and the functionalist ideal has been twisted into an expression of status rather than of utility or egalitarianism. Gradually, the twentieth-century house evolved from its role as the flag-bearer of the avant-garde into little more than a performing media star, much like the flesh-and-blood celebrities that preoccupy our lives. The vast majority of new houses that receive public attention are 'event architecture', carefully groomed like a thoroughbred from commissioning, design and construction, right up to what has become a crucial stage: publication.

The contemporary house has therefore come to mirror social change and cultural aspiration, rather than be a showcase for new construction methods, materials and technology (although these have not been totally forgotten), or new arrangements for living. The modern house in the media age is all about image; a flat representation in a magazine or on television, rather than a three-dimensional space to be explored or, heaven forbid, inhabited. Modernity is what we desire: images of a better life, achievable through a combination of luck, toil and expenditure. In short, 'modern' is further and further removed from 'normality'; a stylistic zoo that draws upon all aspects of the avant-garde, with the only identifying strand being that of a desire for difference and individuality.

This quest for individuality is not unwelcome. As modern consumers we have grown used to being classified for easier targeting. Our lives are quantified and qualified with an uncanny accuracy; humanity is sliced up into segments and sectors, numbers and markets. Little wonder that the desire for a home – that most fundamental of all human needs – is occasionally seen to break out of an utterly constrictive system in search for a new way of expression. No longer are vast swathes of the population content with their modern equivalent of Levittown [2] or a semi-detached estate home [15]; they know there is an alternative. Whether or not that alternative is genuine is one of the subjects of this book.

–

A discussion of the twenty-first-century house would not be complete without a mention of the role of the media in shaping and guiding the architectural debate. Modern architecture, far from becoming a universal, socially cohesive and beneficial movement, ended the twentieth century as an élitist art, a style symbolizing privilege rather than opportunity. How did this progression take place? The writer and architect F.R.S. Yorke, whose *The Modern House* ran to eight editions from 1934 to 1956, began his book to capture the origins and aspirations of the Modern Movement in the heroic inter-war years. But as *The Modern House* series wore on, the visual element became more integral, while the technical details of innovative methods of construction, including prefabrication, were less prominent. In the absence of today's global distribution networks for printed media and, of course, the internet, books were crucial. From *The Modern House* and Le Corbusier's polemics, right up to Rem Koolhaas's *S, M, X, XL*, architecture books shaped the way we perceive buildings, as their creators intended (crucially, Koolhaas's 2005 publication, *Content*, is presented in an affordable magazine format, eschewing book-publishing conventions).

Imagery is integral to mythology. Publishers discovered that for non-architects to consume books about architecture, buildings are best distilled into a series of definitive, striking images, the more picturesque the better. The constantly evolving role of photography in portraying architecture cannot be under-played. Just as the aesthetic prescriptions of whole architectural movements were embodied in the crisp black-and-white frames of the early photographic pioneers, so too have our definitions of contemporary domestic styles been shaped by the way architecture is framed, styled and shot.[1]

Modern architectural publishing goes further, paring innovation back to a simple question of aesthetics, skimming over technical aspects and, to an ever greater extent, over the cultural and societal context of new building. To a certain extent, this continues a pattern established by the earlier architectural 'picture books'. Le Corbusier's celebrated treatises on architecture, form and the machine age rarely included technical plans, preferring high-quality photographs alongside sketchy illustrations to demonstrate the architect's belief in modern design's superiority for the new machine age.

In the last decade, outlets for exhibiting these increasingly systemized symbols of domestic design excellence have multiplied. The architectural and design publishing industry churns out a host of lavishly illustrated books, monographs, albums, periodicals, television programmes and, most importantly, magazines. These last have honed and formalized the system of contemporary architectural representation to perfection. Innovative publications, from the *Architectural Review* under Hubert de Cronin Hastings, who became editor in 1927, and Le Corbusier and Amédée Ozenfant's *L'Esprit Nouveau* journal, which ran from 1920 to 1926, through *Art and Architecture* under John Entenza (progenitor of the Case Study House Program, 1945–66), all the way up to Joseph Holtzman's eclectically personal interiors publication *Nest* (1994–2000), have shaped both architectural thinking and ways of presenting new design, usurping the ideas-based monograph as the primary means of disseminating ideas.

The forum for the current architectural debate has shifted from books to magazines. Arguably, the architecture book has been relegated to the second tier, as either thinly disguised brochures or academic treatises of limited interest.

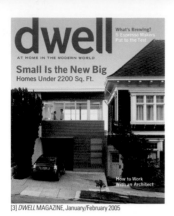

[3] DWELL MAGAZINE, January/February 2005

[4] MONOCOQUE HOUSE, 2003. PATTERNS

Architectural publishing has a mania for categories and classification: modern houses, small houses, extreme houses, experimental houses, houses on the edge, see-through houses, minimalist houses, vernacular houses, wooden houses, moving houses, each a neat peg upon which a number of glossy, even iconic, projects can be hung, their credentials based largely on their ability to impress in the space of a few transparencies.[2] Magazines have had a huge bearing on how we perceive the modern house. The past decade has seen the publishing industry swamp the consumer with publications about homes and lifestyle, a hazy morass of products, places and people operating at the supposed 'cutting edge' of domestic design: *Wallpaper**, *Elle Deco*, *Living Etc.*, *Grand Designs*, *The World of Interiors*, *Individual Homes*, *Marie Claire Maison* and *Dwell* [3], to name but a few, supplemented by expanded home, design and lifestyle sections in national newspapers and magazines. Even professionally focused magazines, such as *Architectural Record*, *Architectural Design*, *Architectural Review*, *Architektur Aktuell*, *Metropolis*, *Icon*, *Blueprint* and countless others, fetishize the single family house, devoting page after page to the sharpest-looking – and newest – examples from around the world. There is also the explosion in architectural websites, a self-published portfolio of increasing sophistication that provides firms with a platform upon which to fulfill their Corbusian/Koolhaasian fantasies.

The leading players in the market for so-called 'shelter magazines', first the London-based *Wallpaper**, founded in September 1996, then *Dwell*, based in Los Angeles and launched in October 2000, mix contemporary work with revisited classics of Modernism. Their self-

consciously eclectic fusion has done much to dispel the rigid classifications that traditionally straitjacketed Modern design and architecture. Readers are as likely to see a refurbished Case Study house or a long-lost Modernist classic from some obscure corner of Europe as they are new work by a young, eager practice. *Dwell* even goes so far as to trail its contents as 'Design for Real People', deliberately diminishing the élitist image of contemporary design. The overall impression is not one of Modernism as a steady, incremental progression towards a true perfection, but rather that the built environment is necessarily eclectic, even chaotic. Difference is celebrated and, most importantly, the consumer is assumed to be participating in the architectural process, rather than merely spectating. *Dwell*'s fascination with the prefabricated home, and even the *Wallpaper** house of 2001, all demonstrate continuing experimentation (however self-aggrandizing) in this field, as well as an acknowledgement of the role the media can play in promoting new architectural forms.

These experimental promotions are not hugely removed from the traditional 'house of the future', exhibited at trade fairs and consumer shows throughout the twentieth century. Despite such widespread publicity, the market for innovation remained small; Wells Coates, whose Sunspan House was exhibited at the 1934 *Daily Mail* Ideal Home Show, built only a handful of his innovative house designs, and the show's subsequent 'future houses' (for instance the Monocoque House designed by Marcelo Spina in 2003 [4]) remained strictly conceptual. The market for self-build is burgeoning; at the turn of the century there were 35,000 self build projects under way in the UK,[3] an architectural

[5] HUF HAUS MODEL HOME, Hartenfels, Germany, 2005.
Huf Haus

sub-culture that has its own exhibition (held annually in Birmingham[4]) and numerous magazines. The commercialization of this movement is epitomized by *Grand Designs* magazine (launched in February 2004 on the back of a hugely popular television series on Britain's Channel 4), which, with the successful completion of such projects as the modular Huf Haus [5], has done much for the positive image of architects and of new housing design. However, the programme sometimes focuses excessively on the idea of architecture as a struggle, in common with other artistic endeavours, imbuing the process with an aura of eccentric masochism, as if to step out of the mainstream were willingly to submit to self-flagellation.

Media coverage might have created a new catholicism of taste, yet it has also redoubled the power of the image in architectural discourse. No matter how unusual your ideas, how buildable your designs, how worthy your intentions, how inclusive your vision and how stunning your site, unless your photography comes up to scratch, your project will be unlikely to make it into print. Many magazines are happy to shoot a certain number of projects themselves, endowing featured works with a very recognizable aesthetic, dictated by the tradition of architectural photography. Increasingly, publications strive to present the 'human side' of architecture in artfully casual portraits of architects and clients. These representations are far removed from the abstract rigour of 'traditional' architectural photography. *Dwell* goes so far as to have what it calls a 'Fruit Bowl Manifesto', a reference to the clichéd sight of a 'bowl of unblemished green apples on the bathroom vanity or a bowl of

pomegranates in the bedroom', and to decry the lack of 'signs of life'. The magazine concluded:

While a lot of magazines show homes as pure space, so isolated from the particulars of geography or daily life that they might as well be constructed on a Hollywood sound stage, we think that the connections to society, place and human experience – call it context – are exactly what make good architecture great. Those connections are also what makes architecture interesting to people who aren't architects.[5]

It is a noble sentiment, but these new interior studies are little more than developments of the formal world depicted in *Architectural Digest* and, to a lesser extent, *The World of Interiors* (which has always had a penchant for the unusual and eclectic and a healthily casual relationship with the profession of 'interior design'). In these publications, architectural photography is the equivalent of the Gainsborough-style family portrait, with the architects depicted making a patrician sweep of the hand around their creations, the clients stiff, posed and formal on the fatally new furniture.

The combined elements of enhanced visual literacy and stylistic diversity feed off each other. As in all image-hungry endeavours, novelty is demanded, swiftly absorbing even the most avant-garde aspirations. The 'modern' or 'future' house can no longer claim outsider status, it is just one more facet of a dizzyingly broad consumer culture, a product of a pluralist age, another box to tick. The market has been swift to exploit the desire for individualism in all things, and houses are no different, sustained by relentless representation in the media. That certain houses now form a New Modern canon is undeniable. Bolstered by their relentless yet

almost subliminal use and reuse in films, television, commercials, pop videos and shopping catalogues, a de facto 'contemporary style' has emerged in the space of about a decade, embracing not just the architecture of the past ten years, but projects that reach back as far as the 1940s. One thinks of Pierre Koenig's Case Study House #22, the Stahl House, perched iconically above the West Hollywood suburban sprawl and captured unforgettably by Julius Shulman in his 1960 photograph.[6] It is an image that has been endlessly recycled; at the end of 2004 it was visible in billboard adverts for beer, several pop videos, photoshoots and even as a location in a computer game. Countless variations have gone before it. But even Shulman's pictures, which appear to depict honestly the nascent 1960s fascination with modern architecture, were utterly staged, setting up the unattainable image of perfection. 'There was a lot of improvization, cutting branches and moving them to hide bare spots or create the illusion of land where it didn't exist,' recalled Shulman's assistant Leland Y. Lee in 2001.[7]

Shulman is far from alone in treating freshly completed architecture as a stage set that can be moulded and dressed to portray a higher truth. It is universal within architectural photography; few of the pictures in this book have escaped, in some form or another, being 'styled'. For dwellings that double up as (high-earning) media stars, such duality is almost built into the original brief. Graham Phillips's Skywood House (1998), in Middlesex, England, swiftly became a favourite location for advertisers and fashion shoots, selling everything from sofas to sporting hatchbacks, cropping up again and again behind the new season's colours or

shapes [6].[8] Copyright, that bugbear of architectural publishing, precludes their reproduction here, but the existence of such companies as Lavish Locations (which has more than 100 'minimal and high-tech' properties and nearly 350 'modern' family properties on its books) is evidence of a huge media demand for contemporary domestic imagery.[9] It helps, of course, that Modernism's reductivist tendencies create perfect canvases, blank spaces that are ready-made for the stylist's art. A series of minimally furnished public rooms, backed by smaller, less visible private areas that are also handy places to shovel the detritus of day-to-day life when the photographers come round, the New Modern house presents itself as a stage set as much as a domestic setting.

Architectural representation has always been dishonest, and houses, perhaps more than any other typology, are the most dishonestly represented of all. As Jonathan Hill noted in his essay on the original images of Mies van der Rohe's Barcelona Pavilion (1929) in the anthology *This Is Not Architecture*, 'the history of the Pavilion implied that contemplation is the experience most appropriate to buildings, affirming the authority of the architect and denying that of the user'.[10] Look but don't touch. This is perhaps the overriding message that seeps from the pages of architectural publishing and through the glossy perfection of the media-savvy house; that in the twenty-first century, modern architecture – that is to say, architecture that somehow transcends the everyday – is somehow more meditative and prescriptive in the way it should be approached and experienced. That architects should so frequently trot out the desire to 'maximize space and light' is merely another manifestation of

architecture's elevated sense of self-importance. All too often, actual *living* does not get a look-in.

Ironically for architects, and despite their powers of self-promotion and self-mythology, the high profile of what one could accurately term New Contemporary Style has come about almost entirely independently of their seven decades of propaganda and stylistic strictures. It is almost as if New Contemporary has evolved into the manufactured boy-band of the architecture world, an immaculately conceived glossy image that no one, at heart, takes terribly seriously. These houses are not the real world. And where, in all this innovation and perfectionism, is the mass market? Despite growing affection for contemporary architecture, and perhaps a sneaking admiration for the toned lines of the New Contemporary Style, time and time again the public demonstrates a desire for the traditional and the known over the avant-garde. IKEA's early 1990s exhortations to 'chuck out your chintz' were swiftly forgotten in the furniture giant's subsequent decision to flood the market with floral and patterned fabrics. A certain section of society will always like to keep strange architecture firmly where it belongs, as a subject for suburban outrage on television programmes such as *Changing Rooms*, as the eccentric predilections of moneyed egoists on *Grand Designs*, or even as the strangely exotic gilded cage for the freaks and extroverts of *Big Brother*. For many, these are the places where modern residential architecture truly belongs; an unattainable elsewhere that has little to do with their day-to-day life.

—

So is there an archetypal twenty-first-century house? No: there are many. This book identifies four themes: iconic houses in the landscape, new urban sites, new pragmatic architecture, and future concepts; but there could just as easily be 100 such distinctions. These categories are little more than classifying snapshots, illustrating existing and emerging future directions for house design. They are not ground-breaking in their scope, for new housing archetypes are largely imaginary.

The first section, The Iconic House, presents 16 contemporary houses in the grand Modernist tradition. There will always be a place for the stand-alone contemporary house, the statement that stands deliberately apart from the landscape (or, alternatively, works in harmony with it). The modern age has seen the emergence of the media-savvy practice, aware of the role that image has to play in disseminating its ideas to a wider audience, and therefore reaching more clients. Increasingly, it is the presentation of a project, be it to potential clients, the public at large or legislative bodies, that decides its future, and the past decade has seen a dramatic escalation in the role of computer-generated images in the public debate about architecture. This does not apply just to big public projects, but to all scales of architecture, including the single family house. In *Is It All About Image?*[11] the architectural PR and author Laura Iloniemi describes the strategy prepared for the launch of Ushida Findlay's Grafton New Hall [7], a speculative house design for a site in Cheshire, England, on the initiative of developer Ferrario Burns Hood.[12] Grafton New Hall, a dramatic starfish-shaped structure pitched at individualist millionaires, might have been included in a book such as this, had the project eventually been constructed (although this is still a possibility). What emerged was the sense that, despite architect Kathryn Findlay's obvious capabilities,

[8] POOLHOUSE, Sagaponac, New York, USA, 2000. Lindy Roy

[9] SHELTER ISLAND PAVILION, New York, USA, 2001.
Stamberg Aferiat Architecture

[10] ABANDONED TERRACES, County Durham, UK

[11] VERTICAL HOUSE, Los Angeles, USA, 2003. Lorcan O'Herlihy
Architects

here was an entirely new form of architectural patronage, buoyed by the twin idols of celebrity and image. Instead of tailoring the modern house to the client in the time-honoured architectural tradition, new architecture, in league with powerful PR and image generation, is providing itself as a ready-made design, a 'designer' object.

That future has already arrived in the form of speculative housing estates being constructed by an invited group of prominent architects at Sagaponac in New York's Hamptons [8], and even larger individual projects such as Campbell Cliffs in Tucson, Arizona by Les Wallach of Line and Space Architects (see pp.78–81). These schemes commodify 'modern design' as an exclusive, upmarket product, but a quick look around property supplements reveals that the term is so broad as to be denied any real meaning. Such projects as the vast Palm Islands developments in Dubai – Jebel Ali, Jumeirah and Deira – are no less 'modern', predicated entirely on CGI (computer-generated imagery), with the supposed delights and attractions awaiting prospective purchasers listed in glossy brochures. Such 'virtual architecture' [9] has become common currency in the architectural press and publishing industry, which increasingly operates a policy of 'only the strong will survive'. In the world of the high-resolution render, modesty, refinement and sobriety are in short supply. Architect-designed developments are led by names, not buildings – a Foster apartment block, a Murcutt or Siza villa in the sun, a Meier beach house.

The second section deals with new urban sites. While the speculative housing of the eighteenth and nineteenth centuries focused on a formal urbanism, the twentieth century was characterized by new horizons, the push for suburbia, the fragmentation of dense, clustered housing such as the terrace [10] in favour of the individual plot, if not the individualist design. The twenty-first century lacks such programmatic certainties. A new stand-alone, single family house is as likely to be built on a third-hand suburban plot as on a virgin site in open country; in cities worldwide, there is a paucity of suitable inner-city plots. That has not stopped many contemporary architects – and strong-minded clients – from striving for a new form of urban residential architecture, combining the pragmatism demonstrated in the book's third section with the stylistic and technological innovations of the early Modern era [11]. The section also contrasts the constant renewal of the urban fabric in such a city as Tokyo with the bureacratic complexities and hard-won aesthetic struggle of building on a small site in a city such as London or Paris, where urban sites are frequently remnants of nineteenth- and twentieth-century urbanism, a patchwork of left-over plots and overlooked spaces.

Perhaps it is a sign of cultural maturity that far from all the houses featured in this book claim to be changing the world with their radical stance or technological innovation. The book's third section, The Practical House, covers an emerging residential tradition that eschews photogenic glamour in favour of pragmatism and practicality, reassessing and re-presenting residential design according to the ways in which we actually live, as opposed to creating statements based on a perceived 'lifestyle' or expressing an ultra-formal aesthetic approach. New Pragmatic architecture often, though not always, has its roots in a vernacular tradition, though more frequently, and appropriately, it is

[12] FLATPAK HOUSE, 2005. Lazor Office

[13] PROPOSITION FOR SUBURBAN LIVING, Raleigh, North Carolina, USA, 2003. Borden Partnership

[14] 2.1 HOUSE, Berkeley, USA, 2005. Iwamoto Scott Architecture

concerned with affordable building solutions, self-build simplicity in place of unnecessary complexity [12]. Ironically, one of the characteristics of New Pragmatism is its willingness to indulge in material and structural experimentation, as well as placing overt emphasis on environmentally sound methods of construction and living systems. For this reason, the houses and housing in this section are often the most politically and socially persuasive projects in the book; these are the architects and designers willing to tackle the vital concerns of the age.

The fourth and final section is perhaps the most conventionally structured section of the book. In it is presented a series of visions, some humble, some high-minded, for tomorrow's house [13]. Some of these visions have been built, others are destined to remain confined to the workstation screen and the glossy, nonstick, non-stain world of the computer-generated render. Like all consumer objects, houses are aspirational devices – as evinced by the many tonnes of glossy paper swallowed up by the lifestyle publishing industry, increasingly eager for the next big thing, driven almost entirely by a rapacious need for strong, eye-catching visuals. The concepts and experiments illustrated here certainly cater for this desire, but just as some of the most avant-garde concepts of the past 100 years eventually found some way of coming to fruition, today's cutting edge could hold important lessons for the rest of the century.

–

The four sections encompass the key debates affecting contemporary residential design, namely affordability, availability, sustainability and, to a lesser extent, aesthetics. Visual radicalism, it can be assumed, is now mass-market in terms of visibility, if not actual built reality. Into this heady mix is thrown the question of architects' own houses. Some of the most audacious and exciting new residential designs of recent years have been the homes designed and built by architects for themselves. Architects tend to be mindful of the economics of construction as well as of the structural and spatial possibilities available within a budget. That they also tend to be more adaptive to practicalities that have been usurped by aesthetics and more willing to allow a building time to mature and adapt to different patterns of use, means that the architect's own dwelling is, ultimately, a distinct entity, a fork on the path that does not always give a true indication of what could be possible for a wider market.

Architects' own houses also tend to conform to the determinist view of architectural history, one that sees architecture unroll in a steady progression of stylistic and technological innovation. This top-down approach reifies a small number of key works, whose influence then filters down through the profession. Nowhere is this more evident than in the work of Le Corbusier and Mies van der Rohe, whose signature domestic works – the Villa Savoye and the Farnsworth House respectively – practically cemented the modern house's status as a lone, iconic object, set against both the chaos of nature and the popular domestic ideal [14]. A small number of internationally fêted architects continue to create similar houses, nurturing the designs almost as if they were artworks, occasionally pausing to collate them in hefty monographs.

Surprisingly, it was only in the past couple of decades that critics started to question the immutable, arrogant nature of this kind of architecture, and a grass-roots backlash began

to rise up against the Modernist hegemony. Stewart Brand's influential *How Buildings Learn* is a paean to constant change in architecture, based on the dictum that 'All buildings are predictions. All predictions are wrong'.[13] Ironically, in many countries the history of the modern house is one of constant adaptation, as overtly fashion-based aesthetics are reversed as time goes by, with the replacement of windows, kitchens and services, the swapping of flat roofs for pitched, and so on. Brand notes that flat roofs rarely work perfectly. In other words, they leak – something that many pioneering architects (and clients) had to learn to take for granted (see, for example, the infamous addition of pitched roofs to Le Corbusier's idealistic housing estate at Pessac in the South of France, and other user-initiated changes chronicled in the book *Lived-in Architecture*).[14]

These buildings might have learnt, but the results were not always attractive, raising questions about the suitability of certain designs and the need, or not, for an identifiable vernacular. Aesthetic relativists would argue that any search for 'design excellence' is a distraction, and that history has demonstrated that Modernism – especially in residential design – is little more than yet another stylistic coda. Far from setting a design-led agenda that improved standards of community, living space, domestic technology, environmental performance and affordability, Modernism has, in the main, revealed itself to be just as élitist and unattainable as the discredited historicist styles that came before. Given Modernism's apparent failure in the mass market, and its élitist tendencies, the humble vernacular-style house starts to resemble an enduring design classic, a kind of domestic Volkswagen that is unchanged by either fads

or fashion. It does not matter whether it is a tract home, a Barratt home [15], McMansion lite, neo-Georgian or a mock-Tudor pastiche; the classic style of house, in all its reductivist, pitched-roof, four-windowed glory, has endured.

This is not what architects, designers and design commentators want to hear. Yet the combination of media representations and a slowly advancing mood of recognition and respect has ensured that 'contemporary' design is widely recognized, even celebrated. At the same time, modern architecture and design is firmly located as a mass-market recreational occupation, rather than as a set of commandment-like tenets that should be resolutely adhered to. In fact, not since the heyday of the DIY craze, back in the 1960s, when whole nations were encouraged to wield hammers and wallpaper paste in the name of home- and self-improvement, has so much emphasis been placed on 'design', an increasingly abstract concept whose apparent chief function is to maximize value and symbolize consumer participation in a contemporary, progressive society.

–

For the most part, the projects featured in this book are one-offs, individual statements that, on the surface, have little in common with the oft-reproduced housing types that tend to be built in bulk, regardless of site conditions, local vernaculars or changing lifestyle patterns. The majority of these projects have taken a risk, not just in terms of working with prototypical technologies and materials, but in being a social gamble against the very reactionary systems of home financing.

One thing is clear from the outset: Modernist dictat has failed. There can be no one true style,

[16] PINC HOUSE PACIFIC MODEL, 2005. Pinc AB

[17] BOKLOK HOUSE, 1998. IKEA in collaboration with Skanska

[18] TOYOTA MACHINE-MADE HOUSE. Toyota Home

one 'correct' method of building a house. There are not even five golden rules that all house-builders and designers should be following. The diversity illustrated within these pages should make that perfectly clear. So what is the twenty-first-century house? Is it a pristine pavilion surrounded by open fields? Or is it a modern home shoehorned into an unpromising urban site? Could the house of tomorrow be much like the house of today, unpretentious and modest, calmly concealing innovation [16]? Or will houses become more like cars, cheerfully designed and cheaply built, stacked up with the options you desire, built by robots, shipped out and plugged in [17, 18]?[15] A thumbnail description is all but impossible. Every age thinks of itself as modern at some point, and with hindsight some eras had a more confident claim than others. One suspects the twenty-first century will not be quite so easy to pin down.

1 Dell and Wainwright, John Malby, etc.; for further details see Robert Elwall's *Photography Takes Command* (RIBA Heinz Gallery, London, 1994) and *Building with Light: An International History of Architectural Photography* (Merrell, London, 2004).

2 It is interesting to speculate quite how much of a role the snap judgement plays in our perception of modernity and the avant-garde. Architecture is all too easily encapsulated and represented by static imagery – even one iconic image is enough to conjure up a building. In the absence of actually experiencing a space for oneself, a reliance on photography inevitably favours the better looking, the bluer skies and the most striking surroundings.

3 Nonie Niesewand, 'People in Glass Houses', *Independent*, 13 March 2000.

4 www.homebuildingshow.co.uk.

5 Karrie Jacobs, 'A Fruit Bowl Manifesto', *Dwell*, no.1, October 2000.

6 'The Making of an Icon', *LA Magazine*, July 2001, reprinted in Elizabeth A.T. Smith, *Case Study Houses: The Complete CSH Program 1945–1966*, Taschen, Cologne, 2002, p.315.

7 Ibid.

8 It was this kind of exposure that led to Skywood's being nominated one of 2004's 'Ten Coolest Buildings' by *FHM* magazine in March 2005, not a publication noted for its interest in the built environment.

9 www.lavishlocations.com.

10 Kester Rattenbury (ed.), *This Is Not Architecture*, Routledge, London, 2002, p.89.

11 Laura Iloniemi, *Is It All About Image?*, Wiley-Academy, Chichester, 2004, p.86.

12 www.graftonnewhall.co.uk.

13 Stewart Brand, *How Buildings Learn*, Viking, New York, 1995, p.178.

14 Philippe Boudon, *Lived-in Architecture: Le Corbusier's Pessac Revisited*, MIT Press, Cambridge MA, 1972.

15 James Woudhuysen and Ian Abley, *Homes 2016*, Blueprint Broadside, pamphlet accompanying *Blueprint* magazine, September 2004.

the iconic house

The classic Modernist villa in the landscape includes many of the characteristics defined in the following chapters – an unconventional plan, a pragmatic approach to materials and form, and, frequently, startling innovation. Yet this so-called 'essential object' is very traditionalist in its structure, embodying the popular image of the modern house as an object alone, pristine in a spectacular natural environment. This image has been reinforced by countless publications, filled with iconic photographs, carefully framed to emphasize the relationship between architecture and nature, skewing context to crop out surrounding buildings and unsuitable vistas, and ultimately mythologizing Modernism as a stand-alone statement of human supremacy. In practice, the house as essential object is an endangered species: an almost unattainable archetype that is a reality for a tiny percentage of the very rich and fortunate.

However, stand-alone, iconic Modernist houses continue to be built, thanks to Modernism's evolution into an architecture of prestige. And these iconic objects, whether designed to be in harmony or in deliberate confrontation with their environment, remain at the symbolic heart of our perception of 'contemporary' house design, thanks largely to the propagation of their undeniably seductive images, be it in films, television, magazines or books such as this one. It is rural architecture that influences suburban design, not town houses. Mediated by the created myth of the 'rural retreat' – somewhere to 'get away from it all' – the suburban house, from the Englishman's half-timbered castle to the all-American mom-and-pop tract home, draws strongly on imagined opposites to urban living. The country house deliberately eschews the town house's apparently cramped,

stacked and regimented repetition in favour of a more organic approach, an easily replicable and highly picturesque scene.

Contemporary rural architecture has often had a rough ride, although there are an increasing number of exceptions [2]. Yet the 'dream cottage' persists. In *New Home*, James Soane describes such houses, adrift in their sprawling private landscape, with the rather oxymoronic term 'escape homes'.[1] Perhaps it is unsurprising that the modern house should be allied with recreation and retreat, but the suburban house swiftly killed the country house's romance and entertainment value, bludgeoning individualism via ubiquity and repetition. Contemporary tastemakers mock today's Stockbroker Tudor and Neo Geo, with their four-car garages and gilded automatic gates, as excrescences that scream conspicuous consumption, the residential equivalent of the over-powered and oversized suburban SUV. But the aspirations behind these designs are perhaps only slightly more naked than the desires that underpin *all* houses, a heady mix of the paradoxical desire both to shelter and to display [3].

Naturally, there are still wealthy clients for whom a new house is the ultimate status symbol. But it is not now the case, nor has it ever been, that Modernism is the summit of individual aspiration. Today, as before, revivalist and pastiche styles outnumber new contemporary houses. Tom Wolfe's polemical *From Bauhaus to Our House* (1982), a critique of Modern architecture's perceived unsuitability for many building forms, might have been written at a time when Modernism was the preserve of a privileged few, a Connecticut clique or Hamptons-based enclave of young professionals able to patronize emerging architects with a series of engaging commissions. Today, Wolfe's essentially reactionary sentiments

[2] PRIVATE HOUSE, Hertfordshire, UK, 2003. Fraser Brown MacKenna Architects

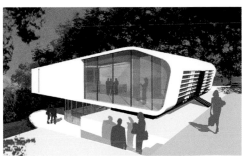

[3] HOUSE NICKLAUS, Sevenoaks, Kent, UK, 2005. m2r Architecture

[4] SAVAGE HOUSE, USA, 2002. Messana O'Rorke Architects

[5] HOUSE FOR A MOGUL, Malibu, USA, 2004. Jones, Partners: Architecture

[6] SAGAPONAC HOUSE 1, Sagaponac, New York, USA, 2004–. Field Operations

are loudly endorsed by a sizeable proportion of the American housing market. Most controversial of all new housing forms is the 'McMansion', the steroidal reworking of the traditional suburban tract home for the modern age: 'In 1970, the average new single-family house [in America] was 1400 square feet [130 square metres]; today it's 2300 [215].'[2] These supersized dwellings routinely feature three-car garages, a plethora of dens and media rooms and an ever-swelling floorplan. Despite their freakish scale and the demands they place on the environment and their occupiers, this kind of house has rapidly become the norm in the USA. In addition, the very nature of the rural community is being threatened by the increasing prevalence of gated communities, which overwhelm traditional town and village layouts.[3]

–

The reality is that the Modernist object remains an anomaly, a tiny portion of the millions of houses constructed around the world each year. Yet such houses bubble to the top, seeding an influence around the world. This chapter features houses that depart radically from the established pattern of domestic form-making, but none of them makes grandiose claims to be the 'future', or even to be representative of a seismic and fashionable shift towards anthropomorphism, blobism, ecstatic deconstructionism, post-Modernism, digital futurism, and so on. Perhaps all that has passed, with little, if any, built work to show for it [1]. The battle for novelty continues on screens and drawing boards, but its legacy will be a few monuments, most of them unbuilt [4].

The trend for the creation of such 'statement homes' can be traced back to the postwar Modernism of West Coast America, when architecture deliberately juxtaposed itself with spectacular landscape for the sole purpose of display and status, a situation that continues today. In 2004, the Los Angeles trade paper *Daily Variety* commissioned several local architects to come up with a design for a 'Movie Mogul', a contemporary update of the sprawling haciendas or glass and steel boxes that cascade down the tight, verdant canyons of LA's residential hinterlands. The resulting designs exacerbate the gimmick status of contemporary design, placing technological and material innovations as privileged devices, far above the aspirations of the ordinary household. Jones, Partners: Architecture designed a bachelor pad [5] formed from four modules, totalling 1500 square metres (16,200 square feet). This vast speculative structure melded the seamless external appearance of the very earliest 'house of the future designs', such as that sponsored by the Monsanto Corporation and displayed at Disneyland, with the cantilevered, oversailing, landscape-dominating boxiness of the Case Study Program. These super-homes are ten times the size of the average British family house (seventeen times the size of the average European home), stuffed full of such dubious innovations as a collection of 'robotic units' to scuttle around vacuuming up cigar ash, mixing drinks and tidying up the piles of fashion magazines and rejected scripts. Skim through high-end architecture publications and visual futurism is repeatedly allied with lifestyle, rather than with technical or material innovation. The drama and invention generated by the works of John Lautner, Bruce Goff or late-period Lloyd Wright have become subsumed by the desire for houses that express a cultured personality, much like a well-tailored suit or a carefully selected art collection. The emergence of architectural 'collectors', claiming ownership of works by Mies van der Rohe, Le Corbusier and others, has effectively nullified Modernism's claims to democratic ubiquity.

There are many architects keen to maintain Modernism's new status quo. The house as 'essential object' also raises the spectre of the architect as brand, and the total realignment of the perception of the modern house. Branding is a marketing device, one that is increasingly emerging in the architectural arena. Perhaps the most naked exposition of the house as branded object is the Houses at Sagaponac project [6], initiated by the developer Coco Brown as an 'ideal suburb' of individual architect-designed homes. As the *New Yorker*'s architectural critic Paul Goldberger noted, 'the goal at Sagaponac seems to be to present architecture as an individual creative act, not as a community-building act.'[4] Set in the heart of one of the most exclusive parts of the American East Coast and involving many of the world's leading firms, the result is not a Weissenhofsiedlung for the twenty-first century, but merely a competent – at times dazzling – demonstration of what money can buy.[5]

Similar schemes have been completed elsewhere: for example, the Commune by the Great Wall [10] is a Chinese take on the luxury and ultimately capitalist housing object. The project's remoteness and apparent lack of connection with the country's architectural tradition, ancient or modern, compounded criticism of the Commune as 'faxed-in' architecture, with high-profile partici-pants retained largely for the currency borne by their names. The bitter irony is that such residential modernism, with its abstracted plain walls and extensive glass, all directly descended from Bauhaus-era architecture, is now a symbol of wealth and status, rather than of democracy and mass availability. Modernism is little more than a talisman of wealth, the iconic early structures reduced to the status of 'signature houses', to be collected like haute couture, paraded then discarded, among an élite ownership of celebrities and media clients.

And yet there remains something captivating about the iconic house, the solitary object in a landscape [7]. Modern design plays deliberately on the ability of abstract, man-made forms to resonate nicely with natural forms [8]. There is no right and wrong, up and down, black or white, with abstraction. Landscape inevitably provides a foil to the object, which in turn provides a 'frame' through which one can view the landscape [9]. These are projects that, perhaps unwittingly, find themselves in the heart of a great tradition, a very modern tradition of deliberate juxtaposition and isolation.

[7] GROSSMAN RESIDENCE, Lanikai, Hawaii, USA, 2003–. Jim Jennings Architecture

[8] WHEATSHEAF HOUSE, Victoria, Australia, 2004. Jesse Judd Architects

[9] HOUSE BY THE OCEAN, Stavanger, Norway, 2004. Jarmund/Vigsnaes AS Arkitekter

1   James Soane, *New Home*, Conran Octopus, London, 2003.

2   Cathleen McGuigan, 'The McMansion Next Door: Why the American house needs a makeover', *Newsweek*, 22 October 2003.

3   According to the Community Associations Institute in Alexandria, 'four out of five US homes built since 2000 have been in homeowner association-governed subdivisions, where residents pay dues to support such amenities as clubhouses and pools that usually exclude those outside': Stephanie McCrummen, 'Subdivisions Impose Social Divide', *Washington Post*, 1 May 2005.

4   Paul Goldberger and Daniel Cappello, 'Suburban Chic', *NewYorker.Com*, 9 July 2004.

5   The Stuttgart Weissenhofsiedlung was a 1927 scheme of 33 houses and 63 flats, designed by 17 international architects as an 'ideal suburb' for the Deutsche Werkbund exhibition.

[10] SUITCASE HOUSE, Commune by the Great Wall, China, 2000–2. EDGE Design Institute, SOHO CHINA

1   The house has a spectacular site, perched
    high on the cliffs overlooking the South
    Pacific. Slender glass balustrades shield the
    walkway along the front.
2   Viewed from the ocean, the sheer scale of the
    cliffs is apparent. The white walls and large
    expanse of glass make an unapologetically
    bold statement.

DOVER HEIGHTS HOUSE

Sydney, Australia

2003

Walters and Cohen

2

The Modernist beachside villa was
popularized by the work of architects
in California and upstate New York,
where beachside living found easy
expression in the aesthetic of white
walls, angular geometries and
extensive glazing. Although these
houses were often built of timber,
rather than the favoured materials
of concrete and steel, the effect was
the same.

The edge of the South Pacific,
where Sydney crumbles into the
curving expanse of Bondi Beach,
has not been similarly blessed with
interesting architecture; the city's
suburban villas have simply spread
to the clifftops, with little indication
of the panoramic vistas beneath.
The view was a primary consideration
in this new beach house by the
London-based firm of Walters and
Cohen (constructed in conjunction
with the New South Wales firm
Collins and Turner), yet the house is
arranged so as to conceal the vista
from the approach.

The house is located on a tight
site perched atop a sandstone cliff,
80 metres (260 feet) above the
waves. On entering, one steps into
an 8-metre (26-foot) high triangular
foyer, which occupies the slot
between the two slightly offset
rectangles that form the house. One
of these contains sleeping areas on

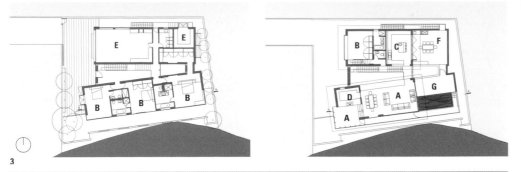

3   Ground- and first-floor plans. The plan is
arranged as two offset rectangles, with
circulation contained within: [A] living room,
[B] bedroom, [C] kitchen, [D] studio,
[E] garage/utility, [F] upper garden,
[G] pool and deck.
4   Seafront elevation. Extensively glazed to make
the most of the views, the bedrooms are
located on the lower floors, with the living
rooms above.
5   The living room, with its view over the
first-floor pool, melting into the ocean beyond.
Clerestory windows maximize high-level light.
6   The master bedroom, illustrating the extent
to which extraneous detailing has been
stripped out.

3

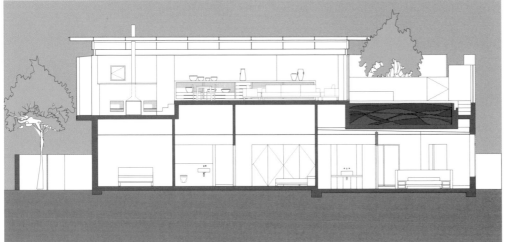

4

the ground floor, with living space above. The other contains the garage, services and a kitchen/diner. An interlinked terrace at first-floor level forms an upper deck, with a small pool, accessed from folding sliding doors. The kitchen terrace includes a 6-metre (20-foot) mature tree, craned into the site once building works had finished. A small external courtyard is sunk into the heart of the plan, at the point where the two 'boxes' pivot apart.

Materials and finishes are luxurious, from recycled Australian jarrah hardwood to blue limestone and polished concrete, all designed to set off a copious art collection.

Detailing is minimal and refined, including a cantilevered 'floating' staircase in the main foyer. As one might expect, the seaward façade is largely glazed, and from the living area one looks out across the pool past a glass windbreak to the view. Handrails are clear, frameless glass. Clerestory windows in the upper living rooms provide additional daylight. While the three bedrooms on the ground floor have handsome views of their own, the vista is shielded from the entrance hall. It is only on ascending the stairs that the endless horizon is revealed.

The views from the upper floor, terrace and pool are vertiginous,

practically defying visitors to stand at the edge – the upper storey oversails the lower one by a few feet. At ground-floor level a path runs right in front of the house, along the very top of the cliff. The overall building area is relatively small – 320 square metres (3450 square feet) – but the quality of materials and, above all, the site, meant that an ultra-low-cost solution was never a practical proposition. The architecture of Dover Heights does not have to work hard for effect: the emphasis is instead on careful detailing and meticulous construction, allowing the views to speak for themselves.

5

6

1

2

HAUS NAIRZ

St Georgen, Oberösterreich, Austria

2000

Gärtner & Neururer

1 The Haus Nairz, viewed from the meadow. A long, slender box, wood-clad in the manner of a traditional chalet yet nakedly modern.

2 The south façade of the house, divided into four individual sections, modulated with almost typographic elements.

3 The ground-floor living area runs across two of the 'bays', with a void to the floor above.

4 The kitchen, in the heart of the house, is based around a central island unit.

5 The master bathroom. The modular design of the house is reflected in the custom-built cabinets surrounding the mirror.

6 Section through the house, showing the circulation pushed to the rear of the plan, along with service areas, maximizing the available floor space.

3

4

5

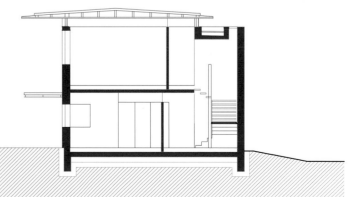

6

7   The ground- and first-floor plans illustrate
    how each function is contained within its
    own section: [A] living room, [B] bedroom,
    [C] kitchen, [D] studio, [E] recreation/utility,
    [F] bathroom, [G] dining room, [H] patio.
8   Façade detail, with windows set back behind
    finely resolved wooden cladding.

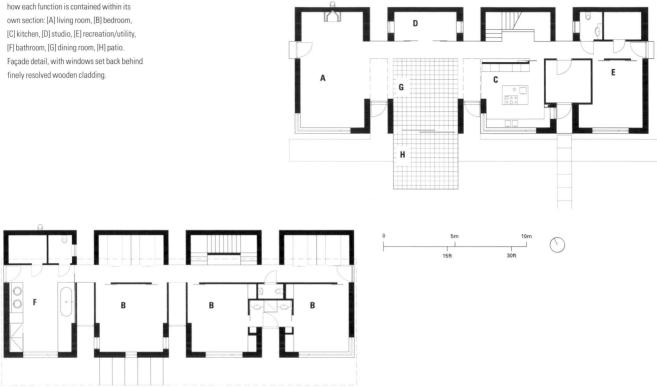

7

The Haus Nairz takes the shape of four small pavilions, or a compact terrace of tightly abutting dwellings. In reality, this single family house is a carefully composed series of four sections, oriented so as to make the most of an unpromising site, bounded by a factory to the north. The south façade is given the full expressive treatment, with an almost typographical arrangement of larch-clad elements, repeated and rotated to form a bold pattern. In contrast, the north façade is plastered and painted red and kept almost completely free of fenestration; a series of three 'viewing slots', marking the space

between each component, overlooks the industrial zone, which is echoed by the stainless-steel chimney flue rising up to the west of the property.

The south façade's windows, which overlook a meadow, vary according to the function of the room. The four first-floor elements are united by a corridor running the length of the house. Two children's rooms, connected by a shared shower-room, occupy the front bays on the east side, with a staircase ascending one rear bay and a large walk-in storage area occupying the other. The parents have the other side of the house, with an en-suite

bath, shower area and sauna. Two voids are sunk through the house, expanding the views from ground to first and providing a far more accommodating interior than the exterior suggests. Adding to the spacious feeling is a layer of clerestory glazing that runs around the perimeter of the house just beneath the flat roof; at night the roof appears to float above the entire house.

On the ground floor, a large living/dining area occupies the building's west side, with sliding doors opening the dining area out to the garden. The kitchen is placed at the heart of the house. Fixtures and

fittings are contemporary, without being excessively minimalist. The house's modernism is not about strict adherence to a reductivist style; instead, it takes the abstraction and simplicity of the contemporary visual vocabulary and applies them to a difficult site. This is the true legacy of Modernism – that modern architecture should exploit the material, technological and geographical situation to make the very best of the situation.

ROCHMAN RESIDENCE

Pacific Palisades, California, USA

2000

Callas Shortridge Architects

California is home to hundreds of iconic Modernist houses, and is also the focal point of an ongoing, active scene. Much Californian architecture consists in statement pieces that elaborate on themes of extreme individualism and status. Steven Shortridge and Barbara Callas began their practice as collaborators with the late Franklin D. Israel, whose early death cut short a very individualist approach to spatial design and arrangement, albeit one accommodating the skewed axes and gradual diversions from orthodox forms pioneered by Owen Moss, Thom Mayne of Morphosis, Mark Mack, Frank Gehry and others.

Israel, along with Callas and Shortridge, was approached to refurbish this 1950s house shortly before his death. The project was completed in the spirit of his incremental approach to design and his delight in complex, layered interiors mirroring the surrounding cityscapes. The redesign was radical, using the lie of the land to exploit views from the 325 square metre (3500 square foot) structure. The site falls away down the slope, and from street level appears to be a single storey. From here the design does not share much with the local vernacular of Mediterranean-style mansions, preferring the more

1

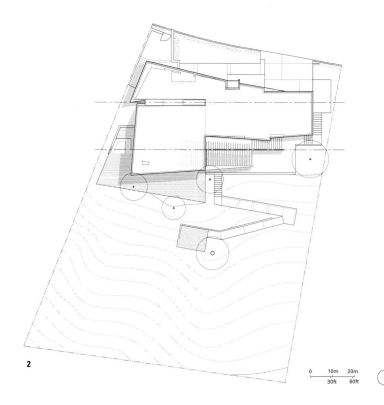

1 The house from the street: a classic view of Californian car-centric architecture, with the bulk of the house hidden from view.

2 Roof plan.

3 Lower ground-floor plan: [A] bedroom, [B] utility room.

4 Ground-floor (entrance level) plan: [A] living room, [B] bedroom, [C] kitchen, [D] studio, [E] garage, [F] dining room.

5 Sections, illustrating the way the house steps down a level on the sloping site.

2

0   10m   20m
     30ft   60ft

B

A

3

D

B

A   C

E

F

4

0   10m   20m
     30ft   60ft

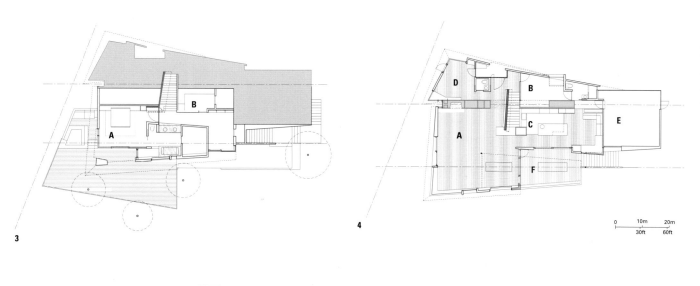

5

6

7

8

typical Los Angeles 'snout-house' form, a relatively unrevealing façade set behind a short, neat lawn and dominated, here, by the zinc-faced garage entrance (the garage was retained from the earlier property). Even here walls are offset and twisted, as if nicked by an incision or folded into place. In plan form, the additions read as geometric shapes overlying the rectilinear original plan.

Internal spaces are given identities through the use of distinct materials that signify various zones, such as the cedar trellis that leads from inside, above the dining area, to the deck beyond. Living spaces are on the upper floor, and where the two floors intersect, spatial games have been played with the insertion of a frosted-glass window from the master bathroom into the stairwell. At the Malibu end of the house, the 'prow', the living area culminates in a bridgelike viewing area – frameless glazing provides an unobstructed view of the Pacific Ocean.

The upper storey is significantly larger than the one below, making the house jut out to the horizon, its rendered concrete walls at Looney-Tunes-meets-Expressionism slants, all cartoon-like angles and chunky, oversized window openings. The studio's later Castor/Packard House (2002) seems to quote European architecture with its slatted wooden façade, yet its hefty red stucco ground floor has a characteristic solidity and skewed geometry. In comparison, the Rochman residence marries old-school Modernist influences (in particular Rudolph M. Schindler) with the ultra-modern, encapsulating an enduring type of Los Angeles design (it was, after all, designed for a couple of psychoanalysts). The leafy views from the top floor seem at odds with the region's famed smog, freeways and sprawl. Having reached this flawed western Eden, why hold back from creating a domestic paradise from which to survey it?

9

10

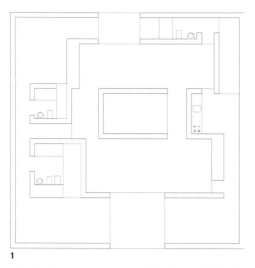

1

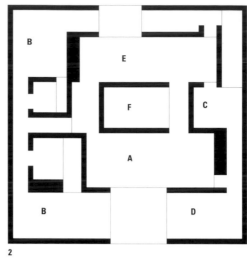

2

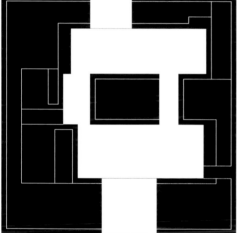

3

4

1–4 Schematic floor plans of this single-storey dwelling, illustrating (1) the arrangement of bathrooms and kitchen, (2) the inside/outside space created by the internal courtyard, (3) the grid set up by the large stone floor slabs, and (4) the solid walls, level changes and views through the structure: [A] living room, [B] bedroom, [C] kitchen, [D] studio, [E] dining room, [F] main patio.

5 From outside, the house is read as a single white wall, a canvas upon which the only modulations are shadows and the large sliding entrance door.

0   3m   6m
        8ft   16ft

The brothers Manuel and Francisco Aires Mateus have established themselves at the forefront of contemporary Portuguese architecture without recourse to a large signature building or a high international profile. Instead, their architecture, especially when on a domestic scale, defaults back to fundamental principles – an absence of decoration and ostentation, an absolute reliance on rectilinearity in plan and section, a delight in solidity, and, above all, the desire to charge solid matter with the energy of free-flowing space.

To the non-architect, such an approach treads alarmingly close to that old chestnut about minimalism's paradoxical expense and complexity: the difficulty of stripping back to a bare minimum without maximum theoretical complexity. But the Mateus brothers combine the historical precedent of the courtyard house with the modernity and progressive nature of contemporary Portuguese architecture (both worked alongside one of the greats of the country's contemporary architectural scene, Gonçalo Byrne).

The house on the Alentejo coast is perhaps the most reductivist in their oeuvre. Alentejo, Portugal's second most southerly region, north of the Algarve, is a countryside of

5

gently rolling plains and scrubby vegetation. The centre of the site is a natural depression, the base of a bowl. Here they have placed a water tank, a pool set within a perfect square of whitewashed plaster in the manner of a Josef Albers composition. The plinth tucks itself into the gentle slope of the land, a pristine object that appears like a remnant from an earlier civilization.

A short distance away is the house. In plan form, the white structure is also a simple square, albeit one hollowed out into a series of caverns. The entrance is demarcated by a full-height sliding wooden door in the west façade – the only

opening in the entire wall – which rolls to one side of a cavernous entrance hall. When the door is closed, there is no indication of the habitation within, and the slab of white render acts as a canvas for shadows and dazzling reflections. On the opposite side of the house is a similar, smaller opening. External views are almost entirely absent, save for glimpses afforded by great glazed panels that flank the entrances when each sliding door is open.

The internal spaces are arranged around a central courtyard, the main living space flowing in progression from one opening to another. Secondary spaces – for bathing,

eating, sleeping, and so on – are grouped at the edges of the plan, buried deep within the walls and illuminated by three slot rooflights. The floor is slightly raised in these zones, with a simple rectangle of marble acting as the signature step between levels, inside and out.

The house is enclosed, labyrinth-like – a maze of glass walls, with light bleeding from unseen windows around white-painted corners and offering myriad paths and vistas. Ultimately the site will contain three more houses, their exact location to be decided by the owner.

6 Viewed from within, the dusty landscape is framed by the large entrance door.

7 The pool is the only other built element in an empty landscape – other houses are planned.

8 The pool is a stark, sculptural element set apart from the house.

6

7

8

1

One of the more paradoxical aspects of
Modernism's survival into the
twenty-first century is the style's
capacity for theatricality. The works
of the more Expressionist division of
Modernist architects – the late John
Lautner, Paul Rudolph and Bruce
Goff – continued a tradition that
began with Frank Lloyd Wright:
these architects built fantasies
far removed from the austere
functionalism of the movement's
more zealous adherents. In contrast,
European Modernism was muted,
untroubled by such baroque excess
and, mostly, lacking the cinematic
panoramas of the American
experience. Formal excesses

tended to be restrained, deviation
from rigid geometry rare.

The architecture of the Girona-
based studio of Aranda Pigem Vilalta
seems to antagonize nature
deliberately, using rigid geometries
that stand apart from chaotic flora.
The Bellows House fuses elaborate
American Modernism with the more
restrained European style. It perches
on its plot, the plan fanning out like a
pack of cards or, indeed, the gills of
a pair of bellows (*fuelle* in Spanish).
The shape was determined by the
orientation of the plot: the street
façade is narrow, while the garden
façade fans open as if to welcome
the sun. Both elevations are broken

up into a series of four continuous
blocks, whereas the internal space is
largely open-plan. The house is
slightly elevated above ground level;
visitors ascend the gentle slope of
the front lawn to access the house
through one of the slots between
the façade elements. From here,
one enters a long living room,
running north–south through the
gentle curve of the floor plan, with
the kitchen and terrace to the south,
the master bedroom suite to the
north. The basement houses a
garage and a studio apartment.

The architects describe the
structure in anthropomorphic terms,
as an animal raising its body slightly

off the ground. Evening lighting
intensifies the sense that the house
is floating on its plinth, emblazoning
the recessed interface between
ground and structure with light.
There are unconscious parallels with
American suburban domestic, in the
neat vertical arrangement of the
street façade, the immaculate lawn
and hedge and the rusting gate, as if
the entire structure was mimicking
the mythical white picket fence. Yet
even the 'landscape' façade refuses
to throw itself open to achieve the
much-vaunted transparency of
inside/outside space. Instead, the
elevation is bunker-like, with thin
clerestory strips above relatively

1 Seen from the street, the Bellows House presents a bold, even ambiguous, façade, hardly hinting at domesticity.

2 The splayed plan opens living rooms out to rear views of the gardens and fields beyond.

3 A view along the gallery-like living area.

4-5 Floor plans: [A] living room, [B] bedroom, [C] kitchen, [D] dining room, [E] terrace, [F] study, [G] garage/utility, [H] laundry room.

2

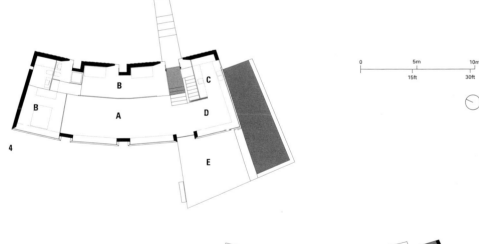

3

BELLOWS HOUSE (CASA FUELLE)

Les Preses, Girona, Spain

2002

RCR Aranda Pigem Vilalta Arquitectes

modest-sized glazing, the façade grounded rather than raised, each angled component standing guard. The Bellows House does stand apart from nature, truly separate in form, the white contrasting starkly with the green. Yet rather than drift off indulgently, in thrall to the idea of the house as film set, the architecture is modest, a stark addition to the local environment, but also a project that integrates with the landscape without attempting to dominate it.

4

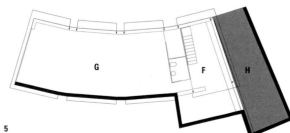

5

SCHUDEL HOUSE

Feldis, Graubünden, Switzerland

2002

oos ag open operating system

This holiday home, designed for a musician and his family, nestles in a steeply sloping site in the eastern Swiss town of Feldis, in the Graubünden district. It is located 1500 metres (nearly 5000 feet) above sea level, well into the snow line. Externally, the Schudel House is the classic Alpine chalet, a pitched-roof timber structure with aesthetic antecedents throughout the region. Yet the architecture of the mountainous regions of Switzerland, Austria, Italy and Germany has produced a remarkably progressive body of the work in the past decade. The single family house remains a potent symbol of cultural progression, in contrast to the more moribund contemporary scene of, say, the United Kingdom.

The Schudel House's appearance on its hillside site mimics the remnants of a rock fall, having casually come to rest after a tumble down a mountain. The house presents two different facades, either 'narrow and light' or 'wide and heavy', depending on the position of the viewer. The façade openings are further confused by the extensive use of venetian blinds, which allow the external appearance to be modulated, either as a dense,

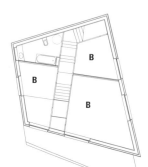

1

2

monolithic block, or as a relatively transparent structure.

Ultimately, oos's approach demands that internal spaces flow throughout the house, each zone 'serving' another in what the architects call an 'open hierarchy'. The plan is open, yet multi-level, based on the European model of vertically integrated space, rather than the more open and extensive American version. Of course, this is a holiday home, and standards of acoustic insulation, privacy and so on can be practically disregarded for a structure that is not permanently occupied. This factor also kept costs down, and the unclad wood interior has an 'archaic direct character'. The architects hope that the weathering effect will gradually help the structure – initially all raw new wood and steel plates (replacing the traditional concrete retaining wall) – to blend into its surroundings, although when the snow falls this will always appear a bold, geometric cabin.

1 Floor plans illustrating the house's twisting rhomboid plan: [A] living room, [B] bedroom, [C] kitchen, [D] studio, [E] garage/utility, [F] terrace.

2-3 The external first-floor terrace, sheltered from the snow by the overhanging roof, offers stunning views over the mountains.

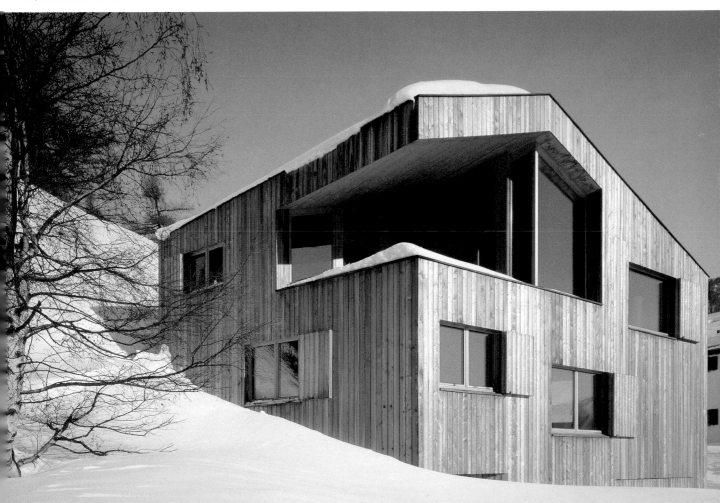

4 The main living area is set into the eaves of the house at the first-floor level, allowing the ceiling to be raised up to the rafters.

5 The terrace, a recessed niche in the façade, is also on the upper floor.

6 With its changing levels and extensive glazing, the living floor is a dynamic, light-filled space during the day and a warm, sheltered environment at night, incorporating a living area, kitchen and studio.

7 The first-floor bedrooms are starkly furnished. Level changes in the upper floors allow for variation in the ceiling heights.

8 Another view of the living area, this time from the kitchen.

5

6

7

8

1

1 The main living space, viewed from the first-floor gallery. Austere finishes, punctuated only by a few pieces of contemporary (but not excessively clichéd) furniture, allow the space to flow convincingly from interior to arid landscape.

2 The view to the south from the main living area, across the Caliza stone plinth with its twin pools; the architect calls the structure the 'Horizon House'.

3 Internal finishes are concrete – a gently modulating grey that matches the soft stone floors. The shell appears almost independent of the internal fixtures.

2

KESSLER HOUSE

Madrid, Spain

2002

Alberto Morell Sixto

Set in the arid expanses of an urban park outside Madrid, Alberto Morell Sixto's Kessler House uses swathes of poured concrete to create a monumental edifice, less a conventional house than a sombre place of reflection. Appropriately enough, the garden façade is little more than an opening punched in a block on a plinth, like a memorial to some long-forgotten cause.

Sixto's house sits four-square on its site, unashamedly different, with no attempt to integrate it into the soil. The only concessions to the elements are the lap pool and sauna, rectangular openings in the Caliza stone surface of the plinth, adding

reflections, light and shadow, and little else. Decoration has been banished, with the imperfections of the great concrete slabs left to define the grid of the façade.

This austere south façade is the main source of natural light, gleaned from the single-storey slot running practically its full width, 21 × 2 metres (69 feet × 6 feet 6 inches). The bulk of this opening is a vast window, flanked by twin covered alcoves, part of the massive stone plinth upon which the whole house sits. The grey stone, a near-perfect match for the concrete walls above, was brought from quarries in the small town of Cabra, near Cordoba.

The demarcation between the naturally planted garden and the landscape beyond is a long, undulating dry-stone wall. The living and dining spaces look out across the stone terrace to an expanse of forest reaching to the horizon. When evening falls, the pool is lit from below to create a sliver of light – another horizon to gaze upon.

Inside, fixtures and finishes are minimal. The key internal focus of the double-height living space is a concrete fireplace; walls and ceilings have been left in an unfinished state, just like the exterior. The second storey of the main living area is galleried, a slender terrace with an

3

4

5

expanse of integral shelving flanked on either side by a study. The entrance is located in the north-facing façade, via steps leading up between two sunken courtyards opening off the semi-sunken basement bedrooms. In all, there are five bedrooms, with a master suite (including bathroom and dressing area) on the principal floor, with views across the stone terrace. The north-facing façade is bunker-like, offering little clue to the light-filled interior or spectacular vistas.

The Kessler House won first prize in 2004's Luigi Cosenza award, presented to architects under 40. Sixto, a professor at the University of Madrid, previously worked for Alberto Campo Baeza, whose early houses have come to epitomize a very contemporary, earthbound minimalism, unafraid to remain distinct from the environment, yet eschewing the polished perfection of the machined 'Modernist object'. Baeza's houses, such as the Casa de Blas, also near Madrid, are beloved of style magazines and fashion shoots. Like Baeza's, Sixto's designs are content to let materials be a little rough about the edges, focusing creative energies on the almost Classical precision of the proportions.

4 Looking back at the south façade as the sun sets over the horizon. The building's straightforward nature is revealed, with poured concrete framing a single-storey run of glazing.

5 The entrance (centre), seen from the basement courtyard, which brings light into the bedrooms. This north façade is austere, with deep window reveals and little glazing.

6-8 Floor plans from basement up: [A] living/dining, [B] bedroom, [C] kitchen, [D] studio, [E] patio, [F] void.

9 Roof plan.

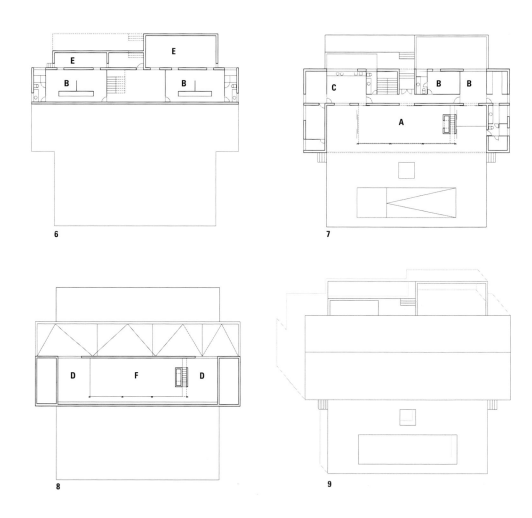

6

7

8

9

1 Schematic view of the garden façade; the external wall is punctuated only by a long, low slot that allows views out and reveals the carefully planted jaboticaba trees.

2 Section view. The du Plessis House is essentially a mono-pitched structure surrounded by a high wall of local stone.

3 A detail of the view into the courtyard, showing the layered structure of the external wall and the beautifully modulated colours of the mineira stone.

DU PLESSIS HOUSE

Paraty, Rio de Janeiro, Brazil

2003

Marcio Kogan Architect

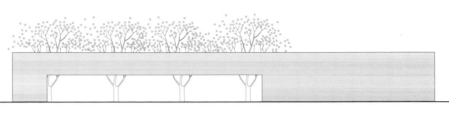

1

This serene residential project is 16 kilometres (10 miles) from the Brazilian port of Paraty, once the main export centre for the country's gold. Paraty is now a popular holiday destination for Brazil's élite, many of whom have second homes near the city. This house is a case in point. Designed by Marcio Kogan for the owner of the du Plessis construction company, it stands in stark contrast to Paraty's colonial-era architectural heritage. At first glance, it appears a product of its environment – a gated community with its own golf course and beautifully manicured grounds. Yet, although contemporary residential architecture can serve to highlight the disparities in accommodation between rich and poor in Brazil, the du Plessis house is admirably forthright about its functional purpose – a second home – and the way in which convention is given a transforming veil of privacy and modernity.

In order to get this minimalist design through the city's heritage bodies, Kogan resorted to a little architectural sleight of hand. Local regulations require pitched roofs – the du Plessis house complies, with a gentle mono-pitched slope above the inner living area. This structure is then wrapped with a skin of local stone, a wall that rises up and above the slope of the roof to convey the appearance of a monolithic slab. This effect is most successful on the 35-metre (115-foot) front façade, which has a long opening running half the width, behind which are four young jaboticaba trees. A cladding of local mineira stone is applied in thin slivers, creating a gently modulated surface of greys and browns, offset by the geometric grid of a wooden trellis and simple cement and pebble floor surfaces.

Perversely, the house within is more traditional than one might expect from such a minimal exterior. Four bedrooms, each with en-suite bathroom, are pushed to the edge of

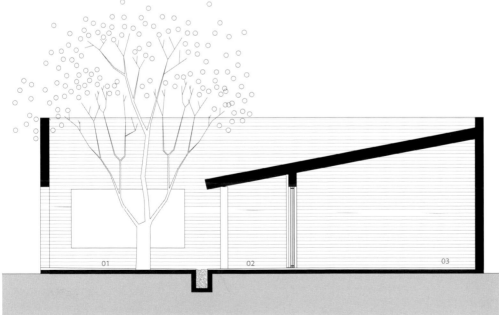

01   02   03

2

the generous 410 square metres (4380 square feet) of floor area. The bedroom corridor runs the length of the façade, and can be opened up to the inner patio, with framed views of the four trees, pebble-dash surface and golf course. The main living area, at the east end of the house, also has extensive terraces and opens out on to the swimming pool. These spaces can be combined, enabling the entire end to become a 150 square metre (1600 square foot) inside/outside space.

For the most part, the building methods are traditional, with curved clay tiles on the roof and a structural core built from concrete blocks, clad with stone. Although the materials are not especially expensive – there is extensive use of humble Formica in the kitchen, for example – the overall effect is both reductivist and seductive. This is a holiday home, a second dwelling away from the chaos of Brazil's major cities (Kogan has done much work in São Paulo, a city with which he admits to having a passionate love/hate relationship). While sizeable, it is also a fine example of how to manipulate space to create a very private dwelling.

5

6

4 A detail of the external wall, pared-down
   planting and simple detailing.
5 The main courtyard viewed from inside
   the veranda, with its wooden screens and
   cladding. The house is designed to frame a
   series of views.
6 The du Plessis House removes almost all
   traditional elements of domesticity. Instead
   the focus is on materials and views.
7 The living space can be opened up to the
   external pool, transforming the quality of
   the space.

7

1 Viewed from the beach, both Casa Equis (left) and Casa M seem to be perched on the edge of the steep cliff.

2 The ocean-facing façade of Casa Equis, deliberately coloured to blend into the existing landscape.

3 Side elevation (top) and section of Casa M, illustrating the way the house steps down the slope to the cliff edge.

4 Casa Equis is the more pared-down of the two designs. This is the view of the street façade, inspired by the area's traditional housing.

1

2

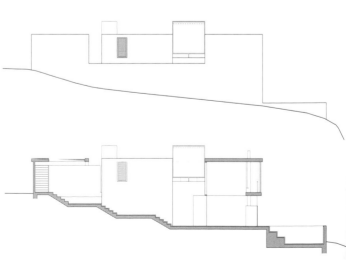

3

4

CASA M AND CASA EQUIS

La Escondida Beach, Cañete, Peru

2001

Barclay & Crousse

Casa M is the third private house completed by French architects Sandra Barclay, Edward Barclay and Jean Pierre Crousse on the Peruvian coast. La Escondida Beach, where the Andes meet the South Pacific Ocean, has an unusual micro-climate: an almost complete absence of precipitation with a relatively constant annual temperature, maintained by the so-called Humboldt Current from the Antarctic. The sunshine is tropical, but the temperature rarely goes over 29°C (84°F).

The ocean-side location for each house is on the slope that marks the end of the desert, an incline so steep that the first house, Casa B, has effectively only one façade, that which faces the ocean. The project is therefore interpreted as a series of stepped terraces reaching from the road to the ocean. The subsequent houses, Casa Equis and Casa M, are more earthbound, perched on the top of the cliff, rather than cascading downward from the road level. Each section still descends, but the descent is shallower and living functions have a closer relationship. A rough expanse of earth and desert keeps the sea at bay; this is not the conventional beachscape with dunes and wind-buffeted grasses.

The adjacent structures of Casa M and Casa Equis take their cue from local architecture, which favours courtyards and open spaces as means of demarcating private and public spaces. Yet Barclay & Crousse is more concerned with the ambiguity between inside and outside, public and private, aided by the consistent climate. Casa M is typical – a rectangular volume, it appears to be excavated from the clifftop, its sheer, blank external walls turning it into a piece of topography. The earthy-coloured walls, all sandy yellows and faded reds, will help the house age in its exposed position.

The emphasis is on contemporary living, playing games with views and frames, discarding the veiled spaces of the traditional home. Importantly, zoning remains – parents and children are given territories, with a guest room alongside the children's, separated by a terrace. The third, upper, zone is a garage and entrance. The living space is double-height, opening up to another terrace.

Casa Equis, the final structure at the beach, takes enclosure devices furthest. Perched on the edge of the steep slope down to the sea, the terrace forms an 'artificial beach', making up for the real sea's inaccessibility; the bedrooms are below. The terrace is shielded from the roadside, and stark concrete framing elements mark a clear separation between the clients and their children (a requirement of the brief). An external staircase links the elements, which step down the slope, from the adult zone at the upper level to a children's zone below, linked by a double-height 'social level' with a large terrace, shaded with a pergola. The most dramatic element is the swimming pool reached from the main terrace, which reaches out above the external stair; a glass wall enables one to swim 'above' the ocean.

5

7

6

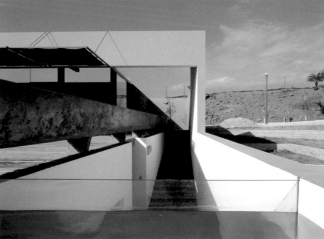

8

5   Casa Equis's most striking feature is the deck and pool, which appear to melt into the ocean beyond.

6   The space between the two properties, illustrating the drama of the site.

7   The external deck at Casa Equis viewed from beneath the sun shade.

8   Looking back at Casa Equis from the glass-walled pool over the staircase.

9   The external staircase that runs the length of Casa Equis.

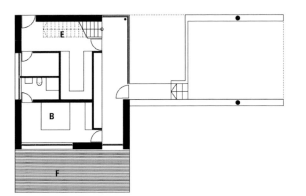

1 The garden façade of the Weiss House, which uses cedar shingles yet makes a bold, contemporary statement.

2 The street façade is far more austere: fenestration is reduced to thin vertical strips for privacy.

3-5 Floor plans from ground floor up: [A] living room, [B] bedroom, [C] kitchen, [D] terrace, [E] utility, [F] patio.

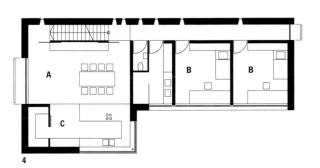

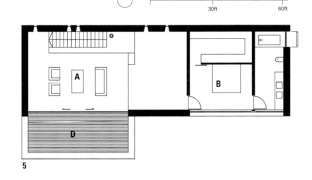

0   5m   10m
30ft   60ft

EINFAMILIENHAUS WEISS

Altenmarkt, Salzburg, Austria

2002

LP Architekten

This elegant shingle-clad box stands proudly in the sloping suburbs of the small town of Altenmarkt in the Austrian province of Salzburg. This is the first major residential project for LP Architekten, and is a response to a legacy of traditionalist preferences in local building. The architects were dismayed by the ease with which large, bland commercial projects could be approved by local planners, yet smaller residential schemes suffered agonizing delays and created conflicts with prevailing opinions. In reaction to the Weiss House's flat-roofed appearance the local mayor was even quoted as saying that 'a house without a roof is like a man without a hat'.

There is nothing especially controversial about the Weiss House, but this modest three-storey, four-bedroom structure is a deliberate provocation to what the architects consider a 'Disneyfied' local architecture. In the Austrian mountains, a chocolate-box Alpine vernacular has evolved, spilling down the undeniably beautiful slopes of Altenmarkt, located in the heart of the winter sports industry. Yet traditional wooden construction methods have been largely superseded by the questionable superiority of modern materials such as concrete block and the steel frame. It is only after houses are finished that a superficial application of wooden cladding makes a rather ersatz link to the past.

The Weiss House uses structural timber where possible, with cedar shingles and larch weatherboarding providing an external skin that will age gracefully and harmoniously. The house's street façade is admittedly austere, with the fenestration reduced to a series of slots cut into the wood. Instead, the principal windows are reserved for the garden façade, where a series of ribbon windows opens on to a mountain panorama. The floor

5

plan is arranged within a simple rectangle, with the entrance and guest bedroom located on a compact ground floor, above which the stairwell rises to minimize the area given over to circulation. First and second floors extend out over the garden and parking space, raised up on pilotis. The kitchen, dining area, utility room and two single bedrooms are on the first floor, with living room and master bedroom on the second floor to make the most of spectacular views. A terrace also opens off the second-floor living room.

Controversy and opposition have dogged promoters of 'flat-roofed' architecture since the inception of the International Style in the 1920s. The myth of immutable local conditions and the desire for a harmonious local vernacular have frequently frustrated the development and more widespread application of so-called 'modern' styles. The Weiss House demonstrates that a stripped-down, functional aesthetic need not be at odds with traditional spatial arrangements and building techniques. Indeed, the extensive use of wood, which will help the house gradually integrate with its surroundings, plus the layout, which gives the occupants unrivalled views of their surroundings, are actually more akin to the region's vernacular traditions than the usual contemporary Alpine house.

5   The car port is set beneath the raised first floor, a classic Modernist device for lightening a building's impact on its site.

6   The terrace at second-floor level opens off the main living area to provide spectacular mountain views.

7   The top-floor living area, with access to the terrace.

6

7

HORTAL HOUSE

Comarruga, El Vendrell, Tarragona, Spain

2003

Vicente Guallart

1 Plans, elevations and section: [A] living room,
[B] bedroom, [C] kitchen/dining room,
[D] pool, [E] utility/storage, [F] garage.

2 Viewed from down the hill, the Hortal House
has a brooding presence, its staggered form
seemingly pitched over the slope.

3 The Hortal House is set within a terraced
garden; the raw concrete walls complement
the dry-stone walling.

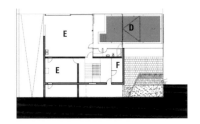
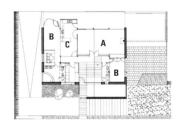
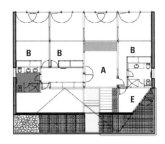

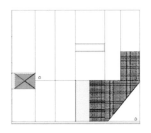

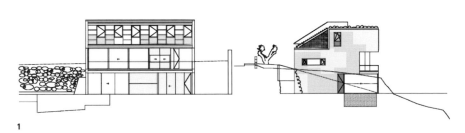
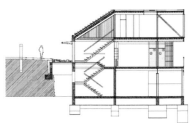

1

The Hortal House is described by its architect as a 'villa anchored in the terrain'. Although it shares the raw finish of undisguised concrete construction, it is unlike the Kessler House (pp.52–5) in that it rears up rather than hugging the ground.

Valencian architect Vicente Guallart's work is infused with theory, thanks to his involvement in architectural competitions, teaching and exploration of means of presenting architecture. The Hortal House is an attempt to make concrete some of his concerns. Perched up on a hillside, three kilometres (two miles) from the Mediterranean, it is presented as a piece of landscape, melding into its stony surroundings with gabion boundary walls, as well as a sloping gabion roofscape. Even the access gate is a metal enclosure filled with rocks, making an unbroken line of stone when viewed from the west. The western elevation, facing the access road, shows the house as low-lying, a single storey with the rocky slope of the roof above.

The site slopes away precipitously from this point, past the small courtyard leading to the front door. From here, a car ramp plunges down past the north elevation, towards the ground-floor garage. Both north and south elevations are stepped, inverted ziggurats that follow the house down three storeys to the garden. Guallart's concept diagram shows how this form was achieved by shifting the upper floorplate forwards like a drawer, shading the two floors below and creating the step back from the roadside elevation. On the south elevation is a pool, the end of which is tucked beneath the house's stepped form and enclosed by glass walls.

The principal elevation faces east towards the sea – the concrete and stone give way to a façade that is 'metallic and transparent', with metal garage walls, the glazed portion of the swimming pool, and

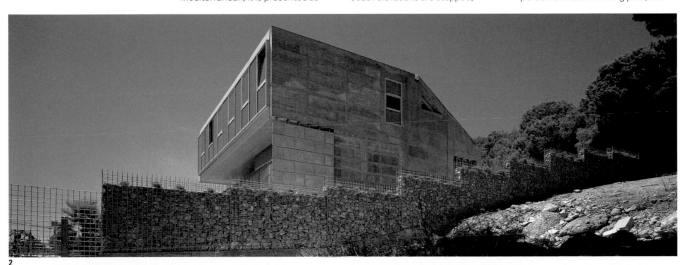

2

3

a galleried balcony running the width of the first floor, which contains the main living spaces – both kitchen and living room overlook the sea. The top floor is glazed, with a rhythmic run of metal windows that successfully brings the aesthetic of commercial façades to a domestic scale.

Guallart describes the house as 'strong, hard, amorphous', a provocation to contemporary ideals of architectural beauty. Unfinished concrete and uncompromising angles make scant reference to local vernacular or Modernist traditions of the gleaming object in the landscape. The carefully composed concrete shuttering creates a pattern of textures that contrasts with the angular form of the walls. Embedded in this thick concrete are several small stained-glass windows, described by Guallart as 'gems encrusted in a massive rock', serving to animate the rather dour façade and illuminate the interior with a peculiar and unexpected quality of light. In this respect, Guallart is drawing on the late Modernist tradition of buildings explicit about architecture's spiritual component, creating an air of the inexplicable that cannot be accommodated by a purely functional reaction to a brief. These are rare qualities in an era of standardization and prefabrication.

4

6

5

7

8

HAUS H

Linz, Austria

2003

Caramel Architekten
Katherl / Haller / Aspetsberger
Interior: Friedrich Stiper

Near the centre of the small north Austrian town of Linz is a dramatic example of how a tight suburban site need not mean compromised space. Designed by Caramel Architekten, a relatively young architectural office founded by Martin Haller, Günter Katherl and Ulrich Aspetsberger in 2001, the house was interior-designed by Friedrich Stiper of Atelier Tummelplatz.

Caramel Architekten have created a house that exploits available space by skewing and transforming the conventional floor plan to suit the site. It sits atop Pöstlingberg Hill, located above and

to the north of Linz city centre, a position giving views of the town and the Alps. The site also has a favourable south-west aspect. However, just five per cent of the available 0.1-hectare (0.2-acre) plot was zoned for construction, and meeting the client's accommodation requirements was a formidable challenge. The solution is structural: a 13-metre (43-foot) cantilever stretches out across the site, maximizing the built space, while an extensive underground component adds room.

The shape and demands of the site dictate the form of the architecture. Haus H has a

conventionally planned bedroom storey, embedded in the slope, with its roof forming a terrace of larch wood. This floor contains the master bedroom, two bathrooms and three children's rooms. Space has also been found for a wine cellar and a home gym. The hub of the house is the entrance level, described by the architects as the building's 'central knot'. Here are the entrance foyer and kitchen, overlooking the children's garden play area. From this level, the cantilever sets off at a 135-degree twist, creating the space for the expansive terrace and reaching over the play area, effectively

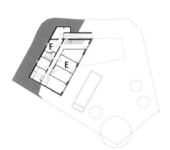

1

2

3

1 The Haus H's offset plan is apparent, with the main living area cantilevered out over a pool. [A] living/dining, [B] office, [C] recreation, [D] kitchen, [E] bedrooms, [F] utility.

2 From the road approach, the house appears as two interlocking volumes.

3 The deck at first-floor level is accessed from the kitchen and has a view of the city.

4 General view of the garden façade. The main living space is bold and dominant, yet also warm and inviting.

turning this into an all-weather outdoor space.

The cantilever steps up a half-level, leaving space for a small living room and home office on the 'half-landing'. The entire structure is covered in polyurethane foil cladding, sprayed onto a layer of Oriented Strand Board (OSB), a solid panel construction system that has the advantage of being manufactured in lengthy mats with a consistent finish – perfect for translating 'seamless' virtual architecture into the notoriously tricky physical realm. The OSB wraps around a steel and concrete structure, with bold diagonal cross-

bracing threaded through the space to support the cantilever.

From the garden, the house looms over the site, the cantilever dominating the view. The approach side is less theatrical, with the tawny brown of the foil cladding giving the two interlocking storeys a natural, almost organic feel. Inside, Haus H is a complex, multilayered space, tailored to its site to such a degree as to make replication impossible. This is what would once have been called 'high architecture', the total submission of internal and external form to the demands of architectonic form. The difference is that Haus H

has resulted not in a draughty, unliveable piece of contemporary sculpture, but in a practical, welcoming family home, a house that does not let its dramatic aesthetics dictate the way in which it is used.

4

1

HOUSE VM-D

Belgium

2001

Álvaro Siza

This residential project is the first private house undertaken by Álvaro Siza outside Portugal. A large-scale refurbishment and new-build, it was built for a family that has owned the site for nearly two centuries, and includes a range of accommodation and a small private art gallery. Designed in 1994 and completed in 2001, it is markedly different in scale and texture to Siza's works in more southerly European countries.

The farmhouse represents the intersection of old and new, agrarian and metropolitan; it is an object alone yet also a grouping of elements that has grown organically, with the vernacular forms of the original buildings explicitly continued. There are four buildings on the site: a former barn, a stable, the original farmhouse and the new-built element. This last takes the form of an L-shaped addition, a principal residence set at a slight angle and tenuously linked to the existing guest house. Together, the two structures form a new U-shaped courtyard, oriented to the south. The roof of the new house is covered in soft grey lead, and the walls are clad in grey cedar shingles, which have slowly weathered to blend with the rough, agrarian nature of the site.

Siza won the Pritzker Prize in 1992, honoured for a 'deceptive simplicity' that uses geometry in a subtle way, enhancing views and internal spaces by a shifted angle or twisted plane. Superficially, the farmhouse appears bereft of showy devices, its elevations embodying rural simplicity and craft tradition. It is only in plan form that Siza's trademark geometries reveal themselves. In the main house, the living room and corridor in the base of the 'U' align not with the bedroom wing but with the existing guest house. The living room is at the northern corner of the site, with views contained by a contemporary update of the alcove window poking out from

2

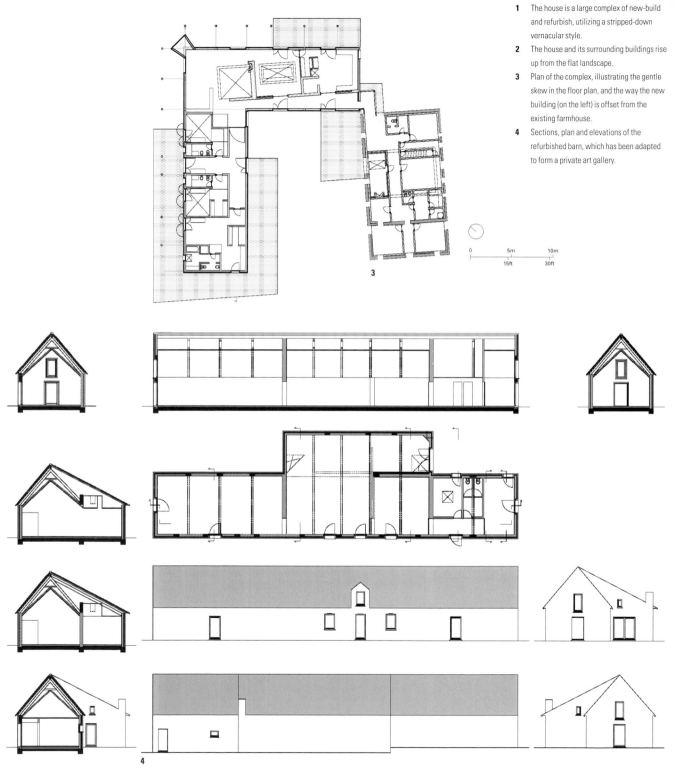

1 The house is a large complex of new-build and refurbish, utilizing a stripped-down vernacular style.

2 The house and its surrounding buildings rise up from the flat landscape.

3 Plan of the complex, illustrating the gentle skew in the floor plan, and the way the new building (on the left) is offset from the existing farmhouse.

4 Sections, plan and elevations of the refurbished barn, which has been adapted to form a private art gallery.

3

0   5m   10m
    15ft   30ft

4

5

6

7

8

the corner of the plan, its exterior clad in light-blue local stone.

The palette is characteristic: greys and blues are combined with Siza's trademark white interiors and the warm brick and terracotta of the original buildings. The art gallery is in the barn (the stables are now a garage), with internal volumes pushed right to the edge of the building envelope, a double-height space running through the long, thin building, with a single triangular void in the roof allowing in light from the solitary dormer on the south façade.

There is no question of these buildings, old or new, being integrated into the flat, featureless landscape. All buildings here are impositions – dramatic forms are superfluous and calm simplicity prevails. The farmhouse complex is about the continuation of form: witness the way the new house takes the same dimensions as the existing guest house, reproducing both wall height and roof pitch. From within the new house, nature is framed as if captured by a northern Renaissance artist – a source of inspiration cited by the architect. Large glazed openings contain views emphasizing the site's rural qualities but the viewer remains within the necessarily more sterile, controlled environment of the gallery.

9

CAMPBELL CLIFFS

Tucson, Arizona, USA

2004

Les Wallach / Line and Space

1　The ground-floor plan of this huge private house: [A] living/dining, [B] bedroom, [C] kitchen, [D] study, [E] recreation, [F] patio, [G] entrance.
2　A night view of the house, spilling down the Arizona hillside.

A house of 2300 square metres (25,000 square feet) is, even in these super-sized times, a remarkably large residence. In the United States, the average house size is 200 square metres (2150 square feet) (an increase from 100 square metres [1100 square feet] 50 years ago), and many special-interest groups have expressed concern about this trend. The term 'McMansion' was coined in the 1990s to describe bloated family homes that eschew design for lukewarm vernacular detailing and emphasis on all mod cons for high-consumption families.

Campbell Cliffs is not an average house, nor is design absent. It nestles into a rock face in Arizona's Santa Catalina Mountains, on a site covered with dense pine and scrubby thorn trees, where the cliffs rise up some 840 metres (9000 feet) from the Sonora Desert. Given such a spectacular site, and such a colossal brief, the architects have striven to make a minimal impact.

Campbell Cliffs was designed – and built – by the local studio of Line and Space, founded by Les Wallach in 1978. The studio is small but dynamic, working in the grand tradition of American landscape architecture. Line and Space's canvas is the desert, a harsh environment demanding a careful approach in terms of materials and massing. Their earlier Hansen Residence, also in Tucson, is arranged as a series of man-made 'rock façades', alternately framing and concealing the dramatic mountain peaks beyond, integrating the house into the landscape.

Campbell Cliffs was developed as a speculative project, hence its superlative specification and lavish marketing. Yet it is also relatively low-profile, rising just 1.2 metres (4 feet) above the highest point on the site, despite the 2300 square metres (25,000 square feet) of air-conditioned internal space (including 185 square metres [2000 square feet] of staff

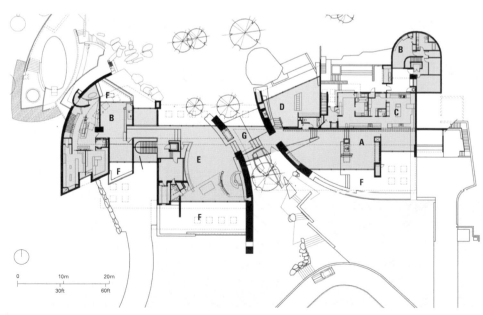

1

3

4

5

3 The house seen against the backdrop of the Santa Catalina Mountains, showing how the design hunkers down into the site to conceal its bulk.

4 One of the principal balconies on the main level, providing a view across the desert to Tucson and onto the house's other 'wing'.

5 The landscaping is integrated with the surrounding desert, resulting in a series of multilayered spaces, inside and out.

6 Steps lead up to the principal living area, with the dining area beyond. Where possible, furniture is custom-designed for the house.

7 The main level of Campbell Cliffs, showing the complexity of the floor plan and the numerous changes in floor level to accommodate the topography of the site.

quarters, a 280 square metre [3000 square foot] entertainment centre and six-car garage). The house has three levels, its floor plans dictated by the breathtaking views and rocky topography. Services, staff and guest quarters are on the lower level, with most of the accommodation on the main level, including a master wing, entertainment centre and office, with the pool at the upper level. Innovations include a seamless stainless-steel roof, and the almost ubiquitous entertainment system. Clearly, this is a house for a very particular client, one of a tiny number of international high-flyers for whom design and specification is less

about style or personality and more about quality of fittings, munificence of space and the provision of such toys as screening rooms, gymnasium and basketball court.

Campbell Cliffs is undeniably modern, but in a style that owes less to Modernism's progressive qualities and more to the seductiveness of clean lines and expensive materials – good taste without the potential awkwardness of the avant-garde. This is a structure that pays homage to Ken Adam, famed for his James Bond movie sets, or to glitzy hotel designer John Portman, rather than to the more ascetic Modernism of Le Corbusier or Mies van der Rohe.

6

7

BERTHÉ HOUSE

France

2001

Moussafir Architectes Associés

Moussafir Architectes aims to dematerialize the concept of the house as a finite box, as four walls and a roof that define the way the occupants relate to the site and their surroundings. Jacques Moussafir speaks of the house as a refuge, 'a time of silence in the procession of urban sequences … [with] the profusion of information and images'. The practice's earlier Maison Stein-Fleischmann (1998) was a response to a suburban site, reducing the volumes of a standard house type to a series of plain boxes, finished in translucent materials that glow gently at night. Living spaces are generously proportioned and

raised up on the first floor to reverse the traditional living arrangements of the nearby housing.

The Berthé House, or House in the Orchard (which has a far more poetic French name, 'La Maison d'Adam au Paradis'), is set within a grove of mature fruit trees. The site abuts an existing wall once used for growing peaches, which runs north through the trees. What might have been a claustrophobic, internalized space is opened up to the exterior with the extensive use of glazed walls, and a single-level, open-plan living arrangement. In this respect, Moussafir's work references the postwar era, with its mania for

opening up the floor plan to create family-centric, recreation-oriented space. But rather than being open houses that form part of a continuum of the artificial world, Moussafir's schemes are about becoming more involved with nature, intended to be 'experienced exclusively from the inside, with no facade'.

External views into the house are distorted by the deep plan, which helps the house blend into the landscape. The façade is clad in metal panels, an almost nondescript material that dematerializes the bulk of the house while emphasizing the old stone of the existing wall. 'The

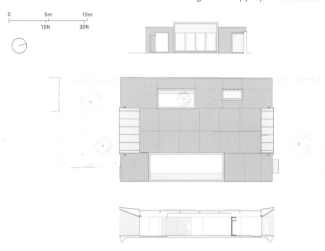

1

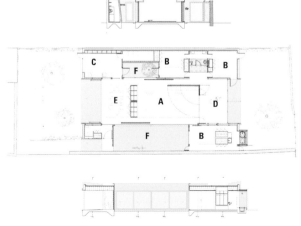

2

1 Elevation, section and roof plan.
2 Sections and floor plan; the house is arranged as enclosed living and sleeping spaces with views out into internal courtyards. [A] living room, [B] bedroom, [C] kitchen, [D] studio, [E] dining room, [F] patio.
3 The idyllic setting, within an established peach orchard, gives the house its other name, 'La Maison d'Adam au Paradis'.

house can only be seen on the horizontal plane,' writes the architect, 'face to face with the sky.' The interface between artifice and nature has been resolved through the overhanging Cor-ten steel roof. Designed to contain and conceal the services, the structural roof also bears the weight of the suspended storage components. Two reservoirs collect rainwater, while solar panels generate electricity. Finally, roof-lights bring natural light into the heart of the deep plan while also providing views of the trees outside. Unusually, the living areas are set right in the heart of the deep plan. Yet the three internal courtyards, all faced by large extents of sliding glass, serve to dissolve and confuse boundaries between inside and outside. Furthermore, covered external terraces dissolve the house deeper into the landscape, aided by floors formed from a simple concrete slab that runs throughout the space. Views through and across confirm Moussafir's definition of the house as an 'inside-out' space. The Berthé House is almost non-architecture, a rejection of structural and material ostentation in favour of a more contemplative approach.

4 A view through the centre of the house, through glazed end walls right along the full length of the structure. From within, looking out, the whole glass wall folds back to bring the orchard inside.
5 The internal courtyards function as outdoor rooms, adding to the sense of openness in the main living space.
6 A general view of the house from outside.

4

5

6

the city house

The house of the future has focused on brief at the
expense of site, although it is location that
remains perhaps the most complex part of the
architectural equation. While the stand-alone,
individually designed house still poses a challenge
for designers, less attention has been given to
housing within the structure of towns and cities,
and how this might be shaped in the future.
Urban living is not in vogue, and architects are
increasingly acknowledging the desirability of
suburbia, targeting design efforts at new kinds of
suburban home. A future suburb is most explicitly
imagined in proposals, such as Gail Peter Borden's
Twenty Propositions for Suburban Living (see
pp.216–19), that utilize existing plot sizes, road
layouts and patterns of development, and overlay
on them a flexible, Modernist aesthetic. Jones,
Partners' SUB-'BURB 2025 [2] concept makes an
explicit virtue of sprawl, by soaking up excess land
left over from low-density housing with energy-
gathering technology. Such dreams of suburban
Modernism are predicated on the continued
availability of inexpensive land and the transport
and infrastructure that sustain them. Yet many
commentators predict that the suburban condition
will be one of the first casualties of disruption
caused by increasingly expensive energy
supplies.[1] If suburbia is doomed, then new
urban sites urgently need to be developed.

For the last half of the twentieth century,
architects seeking to reverse the flight from
urban centres were lumped under the broad term
'gentrifiers', and perceived more in economic than
in architectural terms. The word 'gentrification'
was first used by Ruth Glass, a sociologist, in her
1964 book *London: Aspects of Change*. Glass
noted how demographics were being altered
in the London suburb of Islington by the new
influx of middle-class families, which led to a
corresponding rise in property prices and a gradual
exodus of traditional working-class and immigrant
populations. The term has evolved. In many
former industrial districts, such as SoHo in New
York, or the Shad Thames area of London, late
twentieth-century gentrification is driven almost
exclusively by spikes of media and cultural
interest, with major changes effected not by
individuals but by major developers.

One architectural factor that largely excluded
the single family house as a model for new urban
living was the popularity of the live/work space,
which typically evolved from converted industrial
units.[2] The reality, especially in European cities
struggling to provide the quantity of redundant
real estate demanded by the American loft-living
model, was that live/work was a cipher, failing to
live up to the image in style or scale. As urban
districts rose in desirability, there was a
corresponding fall in architectural innovation.
With the demise of the terrace, it has been left
to the single family house to innovate, slowly
assuming the role the town house once had at the
forefront of experimental architecture. Modernist
architecture focused almost exclusively on single
family homes, or villas, as the generator of new
forms, internal arrangements and innovative
materials. Yet the traditional terrace house was
extolled by Modern architects, who valued its
scalability and practicality, as if the terrace was an
early kind of machine for living, mass-produced
and constantly improved.

Although Georgian terraces were cleared
ruthlessly in the first two thirds of the twentieth
century, they have gradually established a
reputation as spacious, practical housing that
can be easily adapted. By the early 1960s, ire
was redirected to the Victorians. In 1962, Edward
Carter wrote, there were 'miles upon dreary miles

[2] SUB-'BURB 2025 CONCEPT, Apple Valley, California, USA, 2004. Jones, Partners: Architecture

[3] FUTURE HOUSE PROJECT, 2004. Markland Klaschka Limited

[4] PINCH HOUSE, London, UK, 2004. Foster Lomas

[5] HEDGE HOUSE, 2004. Transient Studio

[6] NESTED HOUSE V.1.03, London, UK, 2003. Urban Future Organisation

[7] ECO HOUSE, Kensington, London, UK, 2004. Michaelis Boyd

[8] WHATCOTTS YARD, London, UK, 2003. Annalie Riches, Silvia Ullmayer and Barti Garibaldo

of dim Victorian London which are just hideously dull and soul-destroying, but which, because they are not yet bug-ridden or tottering to bits, are destined to remain for many decades'.[3] Again such attitudes have been reversed, and Victorian housing has also been rehabilitated, just as sought-after and adaptable to contemporary standards. Inevitably, the modernizers' attention has moved on to the ribbons of semi-detached housing that swirl around major cities on every continent: the new suburbs – 'Metroland'. Here, our contemporary tastes tell us, are sites ripe for reconstruction.

While there have been occasional stabs at replicating the terrace's combination of privacy, density and intimacy – not to mention its ability to shape and define streets and squares – the bulk of Modernism's research into mass urban housing focused on the apartment building and the high-rise. Sadly, there have been high-profile failures along the way, leading to the widespread initiation of regeneration schemes. Ironically, a significant number of these schemes propose the replacement of high- with low-rise structures, effectively returning street patterns and density levels to where they were before the Modernist revolution. This situation provided Modernism's enemies with a lot of well-earned ammunition. In particular, the fervently held belief that Modern architecture was anti-social and anti-community continues to proliferate. In the US, for the past few decades, the New Urbanist movement has highlighted the need for compact, anti-sprawl communities that focus and group public services with residential zones, trying to create 'diverse, walkable, compact, vibrant, mixed-use communities'.[4] While New Urbanism has had a few notable successes, the lure of the big lot and the big car continues to be the driving force behind

economic growth: 88 per cent of American commuters drive to work, while one in five new American homes is larger than 280 square metres (3000 square feet).[5]

Metroland clings on to respectability and popularity, buoyed by car culture and providing the basis for the new developments that proliferate around the world. Perhaps stung by half a century of rejection at the hands of popular taste, mass Modern residential architecture within the city is at a standstill. Yet the challenges posed have unleashed enormous small-scale creativity. The RIBA's Future House for London exhibition (2004) included a variety of strategies for building in the city, with designs that occupied gap sites and back lots [3]. Many exhibited schemes were purely conceptual exercises, although some, like Foster Lomas's Pinch House [4], have secured planning permission. The Pinch House gets its name from its tight 3.5 × 5 metre (12 × 16 foot) site, slotting into the end of a terrace to form a contemporary 'bookend'. This particular type of site – the 'hole' in the terrace – found favour with many architects in the postwar era on account of bomb-damaged and destroyed buildings, and the 1950s and '60s saw many of the sites returned to residential use.

Building within cities – especially on a budget – demands a change in priorities. The majority of projects featured in this chapter do not occupy city centre sites, but rather the more nebulous hinterlands that are neither classic suburbia nor prime locations. Projects such as 3+1 Architects' Private House in Tallinn, Estonia (see pp.96–9), Norisada Maeda's Klein House (see pp.106–7) and Regina Schineis's Haus Karg (see pp.118–19) inject the spirit of urban living into suburban contexts, bringing open-plan arrangements and internal planning that makes a virtue of self-contained, sealed spaces. Transient Studio's Hedge House

[5] is a 'magical hidden retreat', a green façade that shifts according to taste and location.

These new sites mean new typologies, for these buildings exist behind a barely discernible façade, with few views, top-lit spaces and linear plans. Few historical precedents exist for an architecture of invisibility. The new urban house is being carefully woven into hitherto unpromising sites, overlooked by virtue of their small size, inaccessible location or the sheer difficulty of obtaining permission to build in a high-density, hemmed-in space [6]. Sometimes the solution is to go underground, as with Michaelis Boyd's Eco House [7] or to create a building that is almost entirely concealed by surrounding structures [8, 12]. Necessity – or simply the ancient desire for bricks and mortar – drives invention.

–

In dense urban centres, such responses are driven by economic and political necessity – recovering the small scraps of land no one else wants and developing them so as not to infringe myriad planning strictures. In countries where a broader aesthetic is tolerated and urban sites are traditionally compact, domestic architecture has more freedom of expression to conform with building codes. The Japanese projects of Atelier Bow-Wow [9], Norisada Maeda, and Masaki Endoh and Masahiro Ikeda (see pp.120–5) exemplify a broad range of urban architecture that does not need to hide behind existing façades. In particular, Endoh and Ikeda's Natural Wedge and Ellipse houses struggle against the conventional notion of a house, choosing instead to restructure living space as a series of vertical encounters, at times oblivious to the metropolis outside. Tokyo is an atypical location for housing design – site conditions are markedly different from those in the rest of the developed world, as high residential densities have led to building plots shrinking, and increasing levels of ingenuity are required to accommodate the needs of family life. Added to this is what many Western societies might view as a casual disregard for historical context and vernacular.

Around the world, the opportunities for new-build residences that take traditional architectural forms – such as the terrace – are rare. The infill site's only competitor is the slightly larger backland lots – typically workshops and small businesses – that have become surplus to requirements. The California-based firm Office of Mobile Design's 'Seatrain' house [10] uses a combination of recycled components – shipping containers – and found steel to create a generous 280 square metre (3000 square foot) home on a site adjoining a scrapyard and an artists' community. Seatrain exploits Los Angeles's peculiarly stretched urban tapestry, and the myriad opportunities – largely passed over – for renovation, recycling and reinvention within this fabric. A similarly unpromising site in North London formed the basis for Azman Architects' recent Concrete House [1].[6]

Despite the urban Modernist's continued emphasis on unpromising sites, and the silk-purse-from-sow's-ear aesthetic that has sprung up as a result, there are still large-scale housing developments under consideration. These radical reconstruction programmes, if not on a comparable scale with the 'slum clearances' of the Modernist era, seek to reinvigorate large swathes of post-industrial cityscape, from the Dutch VINEX projects discussed in chapters three and four, to the EUROPAN scheme aimed at developing schemes by young architects for neglected European sites.[7] The pattern of much contemporary mass-market development focuses

[9] GAE HOUSE, Tokyo, Japan, 2003. Atelier Bow-Wow

[10] SEATRAIN, Los Angeles, USA, 2003. Office of Mobile Design

[11] DONNYBROOK QUARTER, London, UK, 2005. Peter Barber Architects

on the apartment building, rather than the terrace, although the modern mews has become a popular form. In England, the Donnybrook Quarter [11] presents urban renewal in an idiom not a thousand miles away from Le Corbusier's white-walled aesthetic. With such ventures, Housing Associations are playing a crucial role in developing new forms and typologies for residential architecture, venturing often into prefabrication and related areas.

Architects working in the modern urban context are bound by constraints of history and geography, with profit margins as much as design dictating unit size and layout. Yet despite the pitfalls presented by design codes and densities, the new urban house, with its stealth and ingenuity, has become another design legacy of the dense modern city, an indication of changing attitudes to space, money and the home.

1 In his book *The Long Emergency* (Atlantic Monthly Press, New York, 2005) James Howard Kunstler says that 'Suburbia will come to be regarded as the greatest misallocation of resources in the history of the world'. The title of Gregory Green's 2004 film *The End of Suburbia: Oil Depletion and the Collapse of the American Dream*, which includes commentary from Kunstler, is explicit about the perceived reason for the decline.

2 Mark Irving and Marcus Field's 1999 book *Lofts* (Laurence King Publishing, London) was one of the first of many large-format books in thrall to the new quasi-industrial aesthetic and boundless open-plan living space.

3 Edward Carter, *The Future of London*, Pelican Books, Harmondsworth, 1962, p.128.

4 www.newurbanism.org.

5 'This New House', *Mother Jones*, March/April 2005.

6 See Geraldine Bedell, *The Handmade House: A Love Story Set in Concrete*, Viking, London, 2005.

7 www.europan-europe.com.

[12] ANDERSON HOUSE, London, UK, 2003. Jamie Fobert Architects

PRIVATE HOUSE IN SUBURB

Kuldtiiva 12, Tallinn, Estonia

2001

3+1 Architects

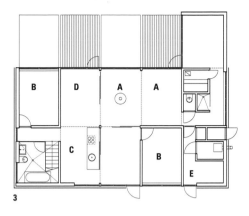

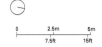

0   2.5m   5m
     7.5ft   15ft

1   The garden façade of 3+1's private house, a rigorously proportioned structure.

2   Elevations and sections, showing the house's modular system of proportion and varied façade treatments.

3   Ground-floor plan – built on a 3 × 5 grid, rooms can be subdivided by sliding screens: [A] living area, [B] bedroom, [C] kitchen, [D] dining, [E] storage.

4   First-floor plan – a living room and master bedroom are the only two rooms at first-floor level: [A] living room, [B] bedroom.

3

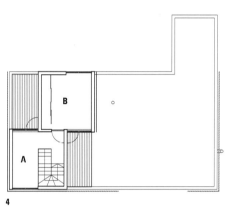

4

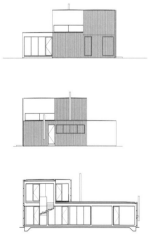

Systems of proportion are integral to architectural practice. The golden section was identified by the ancient Greeks, brought to prominence by Italian mathematician Luca Pacioli, whose *Divina Proportione* was published in 1509, and 'refined' by Le Corbusier in the twentieth century with the incorporation of idealized human dimensions into the 1:1.62 system. Recent technological developments have sought to demonstrate that old orders were redundant in the face of an underlying predictability to apparent chaos. Chaos theory and fractal geometry found a place at the more theoretical end of practice, and buildings

sheared, twisted and exploded into impenetrable floor plans.

This small suburban house does not initially appear to be a strict exercise in proportion. The studio, 3+1 Architects, has associations with an Estonian design movement immersed in the symbolic theory and artistic practice of the Far East, with particular reference to composition theory, an inspiration born out of the Soviet occupation. In the post-Soviet era a group of artists and designers created the Studio 22 collective, of which 3+1 are members. As architects, they drew on a similarly eclectic vocabulary of signs and forms, only this time meaning was

deliberately absented; their projects were first and foremost abstract compositions, diagrams translated into three-dimensional form.

In plan form, this house on Tallinn's Kuldtiiva Street, in the shadow of the city's 314-metre (1030-foot) tall TV Tower, exemplifies the architecture of the grid – rigid geometry made physical. Yet although the two-storey, three-bedroom house is built on a tight grid of 15 equally spaced modules, interior spaces are far from constrained. Each unit of the grid is in proportion to traditional Japanese tatami mats, the straw floor covering made to a specific modular size, usually 90 × 180 centimetres (3 × 6 feet), the classic 1 × 2 proportion. Of the 15 modules, two are decks, two are left empty, and just three are subdivided into service spaces – bathroom, sauna and a storage area. The rest of the 3 × 5 grid is an open-plan space that can be subdivided by floor-to-ceiling sliding screens.

The house is located in a curve of the street, and owing to the resulting need for privacy, the glazing on the north and east façades is part-shielded behind slatted wooden cladding. The central portion of the ground floor contains an open-plan kitchen/living area, with functional components pushed out to the four corners. Only the master bedroom is located on the first floor, up a staircase wedged into the south-western corner of the plan, through a living room with twin terraces. The client's brief was concise, stipulating that the house should be just 130 square metres (1400 square feet), yet feel spacious – this is aided by sliding screens and the largely glazed west façade. The architects describe the house as a 'displaced' apartment, a structure removed from the confines of a larger building and set down on a prominent site. As per the client's request, it is a space to live for just ten years, a flexible space for a young life.

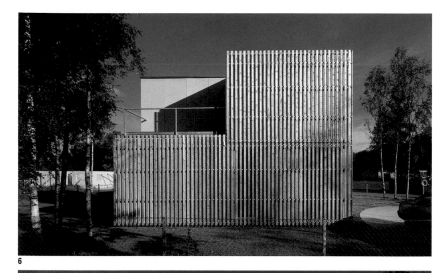

6

7

8

9

5 Tallinn's TV Tower is seen behind the house's austere street façade. The strips of wooden cladding shield windows behind.

6 Screen windows and a rigorous, minimal façade.

7 The house is unusual in that it has external doors on three sides, here leading from the front door and store room.

8-9 Inside, the floor-to-ceiling sliding panels are used to add or subtract from the compact living room and kitchen.

CASA ON THE CAMPO DEL PRÍNCIPE

Granada, Spain

2002

Ramón Fernández-Alonso Borrajo

A double residence, the two houses of the Casa on the Campo del Príncipe are interlocked like a puzzle, with the entire composition of the building generated by intersections and framings created by the historic surroundings of the ancient Spanish city of Granada. The site on Sabika Hill is tight and sloping, with crooked vistas of the dazzling white façade offered up to the town's steep streets and closely packed buildings. The principal façade is four storeys tall, a vertical composition of voids, open balconies and windows. Fernández-Alonso Borrajo created a series of sculptural maquettes during the design process to ensure that rather than 'imposing a specific architectural code', the architecture of the new house linked to the city 'using basic forms and elements'.

The house is a grand urban gesture, a building with faith in its own reductivist, white ferro-concrete aesthetic and the specific aim of uniting a multilayered site with a single, sculptural object. It is located beneath the Alhambra Palace Hotel, a distinctive red stucco-walled building that marks just one of myriad architectural styles in the city, a fusion of Christian and Islamic traditions. The Campo del Príncipe house continues the ostensibly twentieth-century tradition of 'white architecture' pioneered by the Bauhaus-era Modernists. Yet this tradition has a far longer history in Mediterranean countries, specifically in the form of the whitewashed house – the Modernist, abstract interpretation of domesticity never had the same kind of alien impact as it did in Britain and the United States.

The region's blue skies and strong light accentuate angles, shadows and modulations in the façade, culminating in a cantilevered sun-shade projecting from the upper storey. Internally, the two houses are arranged as a series of single- and double-height spaces, the careful placement of windows maximizing views across the city. The relationship between old and new is the driving factor; terraces are concealed behind high white walls to create private zones, with other rooms featuring floor-to-ceiling windows of frameless, one-piece glazing that give views on to the surrounding structures with their walls uneven and crazed by centuries of exposure. All floors, both inside and out, are finished in marble, a luxurious counterpoint to the simple aesthetic of white walls and glass.

Borrajo is adamant that the Casa on the Campo del Príncipe will ultimately become weathered, thereby overriding the apparent perfection of the exterior with its own history. From the upper storeys, the process of historical integration appears to have already started, with a cascade of balconies leading down to the street; far-reaching views across tiles, chimneys and towers evoke a strong sense of being a part of the ancient city. Although this particular urban context exaggerates the historic contrast between old and new, the Casa on the Campo del Príncipe exemplifies the architect's desire for an eclectic urban mix, a city in which tradition is constantly reinvented and even the most dazzling modernity will not escape the ravages of time.

2

3

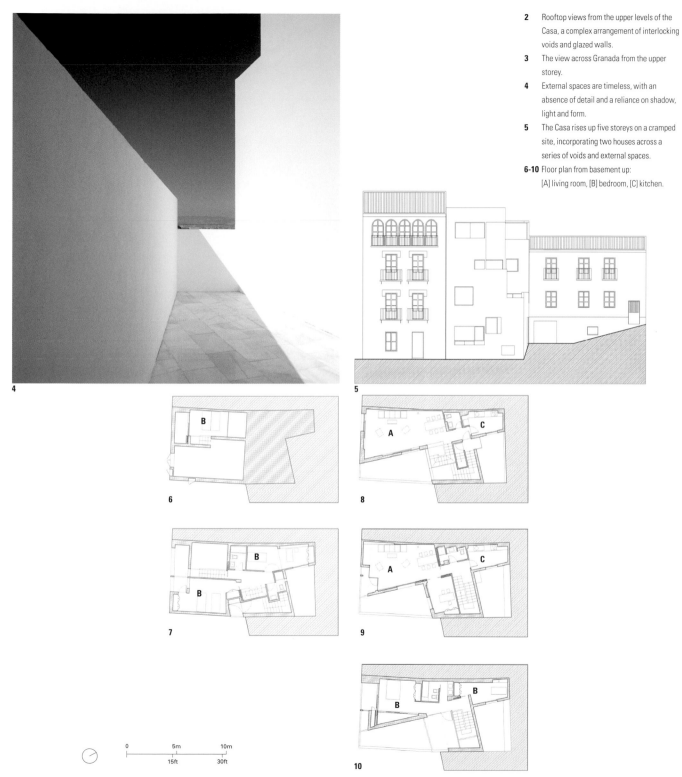

2 Rooftop views from the upper levels of the Casa, a complex arrangement of interlocking voids and glazed walls.

3 The view across Granada from the upper storey.

4 External spaces are timeless, with an absence of detail and a reliance on shadow, light and form.

5 The Casa rises up five storeys on a cramped site, incorporating two houses across a series of voids and external spaces.

6-10 Floor plan from basement up:
[A] living room, [B] bedroom, [C] kitchen.

4

5

6

7

8

9

10

0   5m   10m
15ft   30ft

HOUSE FOR TWO ARTISTS

Clerkenwell, London, UK

2005

Tony Fretton Architects

The live/work space has come to characterize inner-city living, conjuring up images of spacious artists' studios and workspaces occupying large volumes of partition-free post-industrial structures – culture replacing commerce and manufacturing. Yet in reality, live/work is often an evasive term for units that are a front allowing developers to slip residential projects onto unpromising sites, or for cramped studios lacking quality and scale in both studio and living space. Nonetheless, rising artistic profiles have led to notable residential commissions in London, most importantly by the architect David

Adjaye. A new generation of artists has asserted a particular vision on its environment, largely (but not totally) distinct from the mass market.

Tony Fretton Architects' new studio house, designed for two artists and located in Clerkenwell, close to the nexus of recent cultural booms, exists on the fringes of this new tradition. The low budget meant that architectural interventions had to be carefully considered, especially as the house was adapted from an earlier structure, a clock-maker's, the shape dictating the property's width and the size of the openings in the façade. The section is book-ended by studio space – a large painting

studio in an atypically deep basement level, roofed over to create a studio with terrace above with a large skylight illuminating the far end, and a smaller photographic studio on the top floor, with living accommodation in between. The top storey has floor-to-ceiling windows that minimize the impact of this additional storey on the two neighbouring Georgian houses. The house is faced in black-glazed stucco, applied by the clients in reference to and remembrance of the pollution and grime that once clung to every building in London.

The basement painting studio also makes historical reference to the first generations of shopkeeper

1

2

1   The front elevation appears largely unaltered from the original form of the building. The chief enhancements are the floor-to-ceiling windows on the upper floor.

2   The rear elevation also treads lightly on the past; this former clock-maker's provides space for a generous garden studio and large window openings to the rear-facing rooms.

3-4 Floor plans from basement up: [A] living room, [B] bedroom, [C] bedroom/sitting room, [D] studio, [E] storage, [F] terrace.

5   The garden studio room is lit by a skylight at the far end of the long, narrow space.

6   The top-floor studio: materials and detailing are simple and pragmatic.

owner/occupiers, as they covered over rear gardens and yards, extending the ground and lower-ground floor of their properties along the length of these characteristically long plots. This was formerly the workshop, and a pitched roof structure was removed to make way for the studio. The plan form also confirms the enduring adaptability of the 300-year-old terrace housing format. A living space runs the full length of the ground floor, behind the obscured glass of the former shop front. The master bed and bathroom are placed on the first floor, with two additional bedrooms on the floor above. The building provides a reassuring domestic space, architecture that is predicated on familiarity without compromising the need to impress a personality upon a building. It is not an instant icon or a signature piece, but a canvas that will slowly age and grow with its occupiers, with several elements of the original building preserved. In this respect, the house continues the tradition of its Georgian neighbours, themselves subjected to centuries of creeping change, major alteration and eventual restoration.

3

4

0   5m   10m
15ft   30ft

5

6

KLEIN HOUSE

Inageku, Chiba, Japan

2004

Norisada Maeda Atelier

1

2

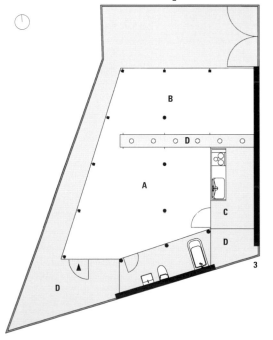

3

1   The Klein House is strikingly simple, with a wood-frame construction and re-appropriated industrial materials.

2   An internal panorama, illustrating the way the internal glazed courtyards allow views right across the living spaces.

3   Diagrammatic floor plan: [A] living room, [B] bedroom, [C] kitchen, [D] terrace.

4   The house viewed at night from the street, showing the translucent fabric walls that screen the windows.

Japanese domestic architecture attracts much attention in the West for its apparently minuscule scale, undermining long-standing conventions of one-upmanship based on size and status. But although the average Japanese urban or suburban plot is undeniably smaller than its Western counterpart, the notion that 'miniaturized living' is the most aspirational mode of living is related more to Western preconceptions about Japanese culture than to reality. The truth is that technology and different domestic arrangements and functional requirements have transformed the contemporary Japanese house into a laboratory of radical forms, untroubled by overzealous building codes and regulations restricting form and material.

Norisada Maeda's studio has completed a run of eclectically named houses in Tokyo and the neighbouring Chiba Prefecture. The Boogie House (1999), the Web House (2001) and others, including the Tango, Knockout the Moonlight and Borzoi (constructed specifically to provide the client with an enclosed space in which to exercise his dogs), utilize tight sites and an eclectic language of form and material to create perfectly tailored, self-contained environments. Another

4

'courtyard' project is Device #9 house, which incorporates four tiny 'gardens' within its rectangular floor plan, creating a series of uncommon views through the space, mediated by the interplay of solid and transparent and the play of reflections.

The Klein House represents another set of spatial explorations stemming from a desire to mix inside and outside space. Located on a tight 120 square metre (1290 square foot) corner site, the wooden-framed house, infilled with flexible panels and plasterboard, has a floor area of approximately 61 square metres (655 square feet) tucked into a trapezoidal floor plan.

Like the Borzoi House, it sets up an internal landscape, created by the dissolution of walls into glass, the use of large roof openings and a general absence of external views.

Maeda has deliberately blurred the distinction between inside and outside by means of a spiralling floor plan that arranges accommodation as a series of units separated by four internal 'gardens'. From the outside, Klein appears as a nondescript box, with 3.9-metre (13-foot) high external walls interspersed with tall canvas panels through which shadows of internal activity can be glimpsed. A slim court runs around the property's perimeter, with glass

walls providing a view right through the structure. The narrow, almost tense, spaces are found throughout the house, yet their narrowness is mitigated by the use of glass.

From the parking space and approach, the visitor enters a 'spiral belt', where the function of rooms was not predetermined. Maeda describes the way in which function was applied almost after the fact: once the floor plan had been decided, the bathroom and kitchen were both left to populate spaces left by the 'spiral wind' that runs through the plan, manifesting itself in the four garden courts of varying sizes. Even the bathroom is

exposed, with walls of glass. At the core of the house are the living and bedrooms, which occupy their own private landscape, separated from the city outside.

1   Viewed from Bacon Street, the house, built from concrete, metal and glass, presents itself in striking contrast to its neighbours.

2   The street façade is a carefully arranged composition and incorporates a large sliding panel for the top-floor living area.

3   Floor plans: [A] living room, [B] bedroom, [C] kitchen, [D] studio, [E] terrace.

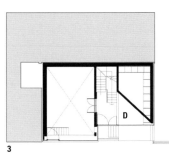

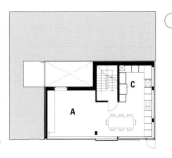

3

HOUSE ON BACON STREET

Bethnal Green, London, UK

2001

William Russell, Pentagram Design

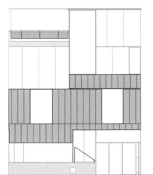

2

This new house on Bacon Street fills a formerly vacant site near Brick Lane, location of a popular street market since the eighteenth century. Since the mid-1990s, this part of Bethnal Green, East London, has seen steady gentrification, as vacant lots and disused buildings have been reappropriated by creative industries and apartment dwellers.

The site measures 9.75 × 6.3 metres (32 × 21 feet), left over from the extension of nearby St Matthias School. Two of the site's boundaries were faced with existing brick buildings, with the eastern side facing a new playground. The principal street façade was to Bacon Street, to the south, which directly addresses the weekly chaos of the street market.

Russell's intention was to restore the street fabric, infilling this hole with a substantial structure that would continue the building line while addressing the playground to the east. Budgetary constraints pointed to a modular construction programme, using a structural frame of reinforced concrete that could be developed over time. Having moved into the house in 2001, Russell has continued to work on interior finishes and fixtures.

The ground floor and basement form a one-bedroom apartment, but there is scope to turn this into a workspace or extension to the main house. On the first floor are two bedrooms and a bathroom, with a small terrace off the main bedroom: pavement lights bring daylight to the rooms below. On the third level is a large, double-height open-plan living, kitchen and dining area. At the top is a small study (currently used as a bathroom) and a roof terrace, making a total floor area of approximately 200 square metres (2150 square feet). The external wall finishes switch from press-formed galvanized-steel panels on the first two storeys to clear and obscured structural glazing above. This glazing

4

4 A view of the top-floor terrace, a work still in progress.

5 The double-height living area at the top of the house, with the sliding panel seen at left.

6 All floor levels are united by a chunky concrete staircase, poured on site.

is arranged to a separate rhythm from the structure, overlaying two patterns and hinting at the house's two double-height voids, 'one in the ground and one in the sky'.

A black Alwitra roofing membrane wraps around the top of the house and rear wall, which contains 125 millimetres (5 inches) of insulation, allowing the extensive use of glass on the façade. A key element to the south-facing façade is a large double-glazed panel, 5.5 × 1.8 metres (18 × 6 feet), that can be slid across to open up one wall of the living room.

In a district that throbs with energy, and still houses a large proportion of London's garment workshops, multi-purpose small businesses were once commonplace. The Bacon Street house is a modern interpretation of an indigenous building type, the live/work space, but also responds to urban site conditions, a legacy of the churned-up streetscape. In modern cities, such awkward, cramped sites are often all that remain, too small for commercial development and requiring careful planning to satisfy close neighbours and local authorities. This house fills its site and restores a streetscape without shrinking from a very Modern idiom. Russell demonstrates the practicalities of a less formal Modernist approach, with façades that respond to the site conditions, maximizing and drawing in the scant natural resources available to the modern city dweller.

5

6

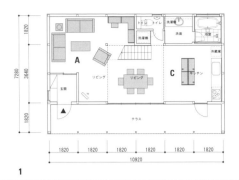

1

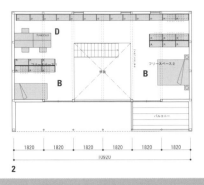

2

3

1-2 Just two of the multiple floor plan options offered to Muji + Infill buyers, as set out in the company's specialist catalogue: [A] living room, [B] bedroom, [C] kitchen, [D] studio. The first floor is little more than a mezzanine sleeping platform, with living and eating spaces below.

3 The main façade of the house, as minimally detailed as Muji's own ranges of stationery and furniture. The set-back façade creates a self-contained porch.

4 Inside another typical Muji house, furnished, naturally, by the store itself.

5 On the mezzanine level, looking back across to the master sleeping area.

4

5

The idea of the house as yet another

consumable, albeit a highly specialized one, that can be sold off-the-shelf and assembled like a giant piece of chipboard furniture, has evolved from a dream of the machine-age architect into a potentially lucrative market for large corporations. While smaller, more tailored products proliferate in concept form – dwell house, the LV Home, and many more (see chapter four) – larger companies have entered the marketplace. Toyota's manufactured home and IKEA's BokLok ('Live Smart') flat-pack house come with financial clout and economies of scale.

Founded in 1983 as part of the Seiju company, Muji became independent in 1989 and now has around 300 stores in Japan, as well as branches abroad. The company embraces all aspects of consumer products, from food to clothing to homewares, grouping everything together in a 'no-brand, no-label' aesthetic. The Muji + Infill house, designed by architect Kazuhiko Namba, is offered for sale in the retailer's larger stores in Japan.

Priced from 16 million yen (£78,000/$140,000) for an empty shell, or 19 million yen (£93,000/$167,000) fully furnished, the house is designed not for prefabrication,

but for a swift and cost-effective conventional construction process, with a concrete slab foundation and wooden structural frame and infill. The dimensions are tailored to the typically compact suburban Japanese plot, and the design builds on Namba's earlier work. The detailing and finishes evoke the parent shop's cardboard, Perspex and aluminium aesthetic, a humane high-tech that incorporates elements of traditional Japanese domesticity along with compact packaging and a delight in detail

The house is centred on a double-height ground-floor living space, illuminated by two storeys of

glazing. Stairs lead up to an open plan sleeping and working area on the first floor, making the house rather unsuitable for family living (although it can be subdivided with screens). The largely open-plan ground floor separates bathing and eating off into 'function units', concealed around the edges of the plan. Bathing and wardrobe spaces are generously sized, utilizing the spaces along the rear wall of the structure, concealed behind the staircase. The design is scalable, with a larger variant offering a first-floor balcony off the main sleeping area and an enclosed veranda running the length of the house.

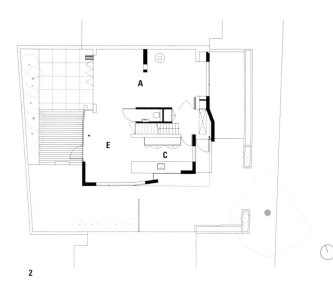

2

1   The Stealth House slips its discreet
    modernism into a conventional context, with
    sharp angles, flush-mounted windows and
    matt black wood cladding.

2-4 Floorplans: [A] living room, [B] bedroom,
    [C] kitchen, [D] studio/bedroom,
    [E] dining room.

3

4

STEALTH HOUSE

Denmark Hill, London, UK

2005

Robert Dye Associates

The streets between Camberwell and East Dulwich in South London are not known for contemporary architecture. The housing stock is characterized by Victorian villas, the occasional grand Georgian terrace and sprawling brick-built estates from the inter-war period. After the war, the Dulwich Estate rebuilt swathes of the area in a mild Modernist idiom, with brick, concrete and wood-clad façades.

Robert Dye Associates' Stealth House is dropped into this mélange – urban yet also suburban, heavily populated yet not dense. The house occupies the site of a cramped 1950s structure built to replace an Edwardian terrace destroyed by a bomb. Rather than demolish the existing house in its entirety, the architects worked closely with their client to design a new structure to wrap around the existing core.

The new façades are dark – a 'black cloak' of timber and grey-green mineralized roofing felt. Each cloak folds over the new house, delineating a structure that has both pitched and flat roofs and extensive glazing within finely detailed flush windows. With a slight leap of the imagination, the faceted façade is not unlike the angular radar-defying bombers of which the American Airforce is so proud. Yet the house is also stealthy for different reasons – a truly modern design that has crept into its surroundings by drawing on elements from all around. Subtle cues are picked up, notably the curious flat-roofed house next door, with its crude deco detailing, and the progressive styling of the 1960s flats opposite. Remarkably, the design drew no opposition from local authorities, who even encouraged the architects to redesign the roof rather than retain the 1950s structure, a process through which the penthouse was gained. The front elevation presents two storeys of Russian redwood cladding, vacuum-treated and stained black for

5

6

7

weatherproofing. This façade is beneath the sharp slope of the roof, offset to one side to continue the massing of the adjoining house.

Although the new house appears smaller than its neighbour, it has four bedrooms, including a master bedroom with dressing room and en-suite bathroom. The open-plan ground floor is based around a central stair and utility core, hugging the retained spine wall from the original property, which is also exposed adjacent to the new oak staircase. The sitting room at the rear overlooks a small courtyard, and the compact kitchen, tucked into the front corner, has a view of the street. The main

façade is a series of geometric elements: a protruding porch with clerestory window, the slot by the landing and a glazed projecting element that gives the master bedroom a view all the way up the hill. The top floor is given over, rather selflessly, to the clients' teenage daughter, a penthouse complete with pink en-suite bathroom and copious storage for books and CDs.

The client acted as the main contractor, collaborating closely with Robert Dye and Jason Coleman on internal fittings and built-in furniture. Thus the design detail is exceptional, even though architectural fees were relatively low.

8

9

1 Section: [A] living room, [B] bedroom,
  [C] kitchen, [D] studio, [E] garage/utility.

2 The Haus Karg subverts the familiar image
  of the traditional pitched-roof house.

3 An internal render of the central dividing
  partition, which conceals storage and
  services as well as a fireplace.

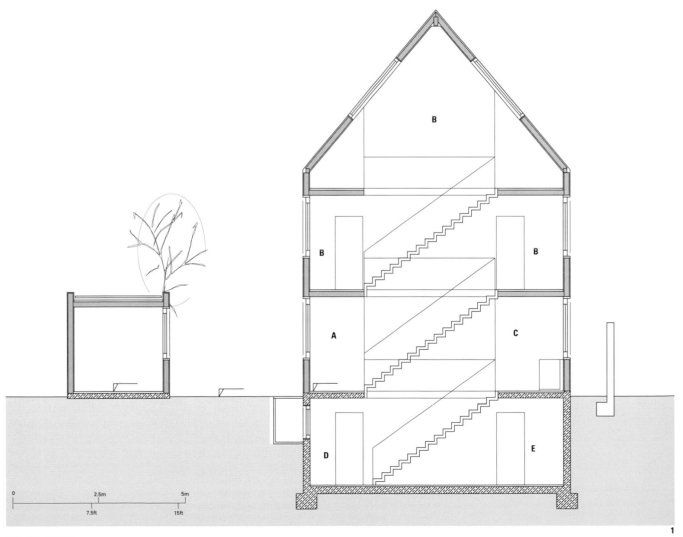

1

The Haus Karg offers a familiar silhouette; a steeply pitched roof above two four-square storeys. Like the Living Room House (see pp.228–31), the silhouette is the most conventional thing about this project, located in a new development in Augsburg, north-west of Munich. Designed for a family with two children, the house has extensive views south to the Alps, courtesy of the entirely glazed south façade, with slender aluminium mullions and sliding doors on the ground floor.

The square floor plan is arranged around a central staircase which serves as the key dividing element on each floorplate. The basement contains services and additional living space, while the kitchen and dining area are located on the ground floor, with a wall of glazing opening them up to the garden. Above this are two children's bedrooms and a bathroom, while the master bedroom occupies the uppermost space beneath the pitched roof, with the spine wall for the staircase doubling up as the bedhead. Translucent balustrading adds to the sense of space, and the bathing areas are linear and compact, pushed back against the north wall. The spine wall also divides the south-facing public and private elements of the house from the more insular service components such as bathrooms and storage areas, and a system of sliding walls has been devised to allow spaces to be either opened up or closed off as needs demand.

The house is of timber-frame construction, with the structural frame clad in red-finished timber panels. The location of these external panels was chosen to relate to the openings in the façade, giving an effect that the architect likens to the scales on a fish or traditional shingle tiles. The steeply pitched roof is a local tradition, here reinterpreted without overhanging eaves as a geometric enclosure that both signals home and is at the very heart of the house – for this is where the parents sleep. The timber-clad façade is also a development of local traditions, enabling the house to be part of the local streetscape yet also distinct (by virtue of its height), an individual statement.

2

3

1

NATURAL WEDGE, NATURAL ELLIPSE

Tokyo, Japan

2003 / 2002

**Masaki Endoh and Masahiro Ikeda /
Endoh Design House and MIAS**

The small Japanese house is fertile ground for visual and technological innovation, without the vast budgets and generous scale often required by Western counterparts. Masaki Endoh and Masahiro Ikeda have completed several projects in the Tokyo metropolitan area, an environment where fundamental elements of residential design – privacy, natural light, ventilation – are highly prized.

The Natural Wedge house was designed for a young couple on a 60 square metre (645 square foot) site in central Tokyo. Unpromisingly, the site also faced north. The solution was to create a wedge shape, a triangular-shaped building with its longest face forming a diagonal, north-oriented façade. This triangle, barely 6 metres (20 feet) wide, is wrapped with a thin external membrane, stretched around the steel structure, consisting of polyester insulation and a layer of Gore-Tex, finished with internal glass walls. These walls are thin but heat-efficient, and allow for transmission of light, enabling the structure to glow at night.

The architects describe the project as having 'no formal hierarchy', deriving its form entirely from the site. Accommodation is minimal. The top (smallest) floor contains a bedroom; another bedroom and a bathroom are below, leaving the largest floor free for the kitchen and living area. The basement has been excavated to include a garage and recording studio.

The studio's Natural Ellipse design is even more radical. Located in a part of the city with a busy 24-hour culture, the house had to insulate the occupiers from light and noise without cocooning them from the outside world. Arranged around a hollow core, the structure is formed by 24 elliptical rings, creating a shape that flares out as it ascends before tapering again at the top. The structure was clad in white

2

3

1　The Natural Wedge abuts an existing building, creating a long slice of architecture that is sharply set back as it rises.

2　Viewed from the front, the central strip of rooflights and the truss roof construction are clearly visible. Parking is provided on the ground floor.

3　Side elevation: a true wedge shape.

4　Floor plans: [A] living room, [B] bedroom, [C] kitchen, [D] studio, [E] garage/utility.

5　The ground floor, containing a galley kitchen and a living area. The lattice floor above brings light into the deep plan.

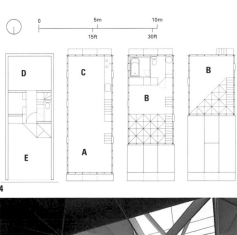

4

5

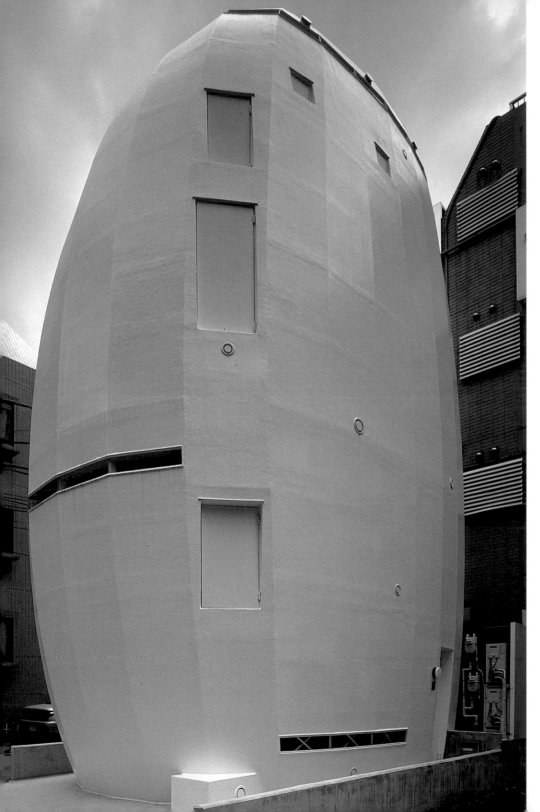

6 The Natural Ellipse House, an almost alien presence in dense downtown Tokyo.

7 The structural arrangement of the Natural Ellipse, a complex ribbon of rings bonded together by fibre-reinforced polymer.

8 Section: a spiral staircase runs up the centre of the house in the space created by the ring of ellipses.

9 The house's unconventional floor plan revealed – basement (top left), ground floor (top right), first floor (middle left), second floor (middle right), third floor (bottom left), roof (bottom right): [A] living room, [B] bedroom, [C] kitchen, [D] studio.

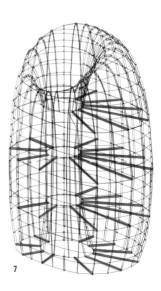

7

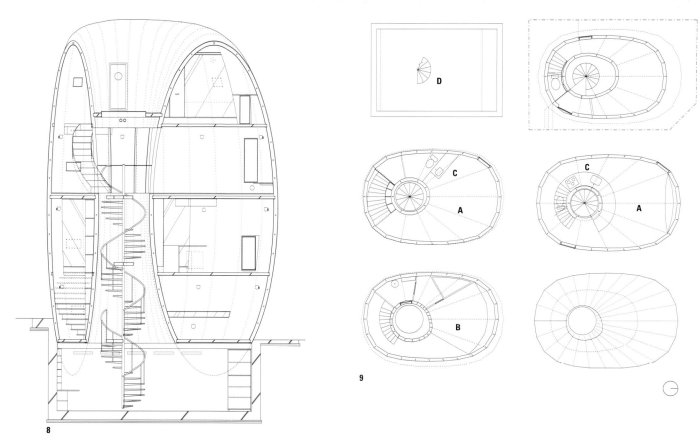

8

9

D

C

A

C

A

B

fibre-reinforced polymer (FRP), a structural material that joins the rings togothor and oxprossos the construction of the building, while remaining watertight.

On the top of the Natural Ellipse is a tiny glass-floored circular terrace, which doubles as the primary light source for the central core. The surrounding walls are formed by the curving structural ellipses. The central core serves as the circulation space, with a tight steel staircase wound around within it, its mesh treads allowing light to penetrate deep into the interior.

Each oval floor is minimally arranged, from the basement study

to the third toilet, plumbed in, rather incongruously, within full sight of curving kitchen units. Two more toilets and bathrooms are tucked into tiny segments of the floor plan. Long horizontal slot windows are cut into the building's FRP skin to provide additional illumination, giving the house a severe, masklike appearance. Inside, double-height spaces are used to create links between the floor levels, giving the house a shell-like structure.

Endoh deliberately seeks 'non-standard' solutions, using computer-modelling and construction to achieve what would previously have been considered unbuildable. The

Natural Ellipse embodies his desire to create 'an architecture of freedom', liberated from constraints of material and structure and providing highly individualistic residential solutions on unpromising sites.

10 Viewed from above, the mix of steel and FRP gives the house an organic, blob-like feel.

11 Services are confined to the outer edges of the ring.

12 A glazed circular floor plane brings light right into the heart of the house.

13 The Natural Ellipse is an atmospheric, complex space. The short stair to the upper storey is seen here, adjacent to the tiny kitchen.

11

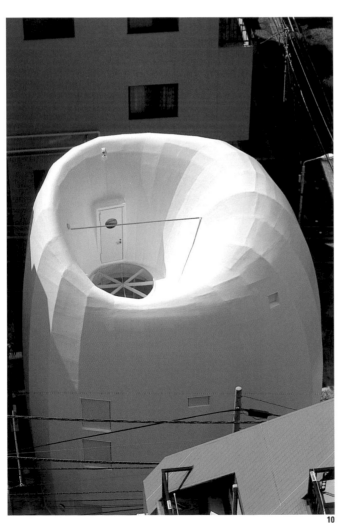

10

12

13

the practical house

This chapter identifies a 'New Pragmatism', a contemporary architecture that avoids definitive or ostentatious stylistic gestures, especially the apparently dictatorial and confrontational stance of 'pure' Modernism and the more intellectually motivated movements that have emerged from Modernist practice such as deconstruction and biomorphism. The pragmatic house is architecture without ego. Unlike the personal icons detailed in chapter one, or the bold urban interventions of chapter two, the pragmatic house is a modest structure. These houses do not necessarily embody aesthetic rigour (although that is not to say they have been created without attention to detail), but instead strive to respect site conditions, environmental concerns, client budgets and materials constraints without resorting to visual pastiche and while still reflecting the scale and sensitivity of vernacular tradition.

Although the machined purity of the white-walled International Style aesthetic seems a million miles from pragmatic design, Mies van der Rohe, Le Corbusier and the other proponents of 'white modernism' experimented with a more 'human' architecture that acknowledged material imperfections and organic forms. Mies's Krefeld Villas (1927–30), near Düsseldorf, are a classic example: low-lying brick pavilions that still have a remarkably contemporary appearance. Legend has it that Mies's clients would not let him use as much glass as he wanted, and he had to compromise by skinning a complex steel frame with brick walls. In reality, the brick façades were as thin as the architect could make them, proving that he was striving for a new kind of perfection, rather than simply avoiding compromise.[1]

Many other Modern Movement architects developed a soft-edged Modernism distinct from the International Style, most notably Arne Jacobsen and Alvar Aalto, both of whom worked with the forms and materials of traditional vernacular brick architecture, while émigré architects such as Marcel Breuer eschewed formal Modernism for a more humane, organic style upon arriving in the US. For a time, pragmatic Modern was even the choice of house-builders, as overt historicist pastiche was rejected in favour of gently watered-down versions of the brick villas and private houses erected over America and Northern Europe. Yet in the end, pastiche won out, be it the hated 'brick box' of the volume developers or even the New Modern procured by wealthy clients in – often highly effective – imitation of the icons of the contemporary house, the work of Craig Ellwood, Pierre Koenig, Neutra or Mies.

–

The past decade has seen a renewed emphasis on practical and affordable housing construction. This has dovetailed with a resurgence of interest in the art, design and lifestyle of the Mid-Century Modern period, and Modernism's reductivist style is once again allied to mass-market design. But while prefabrication methods have a raised profile, the majority of modular, prefab homes that receive media interest are one-off prototypes. While these frequently deliver savings owing to the economies of time and project size, the promised economies of scale have yet to materialize. Other hope has arrived in the shape of the buoyant self-build movement, increasingly visible in the media. For once, aspiration and affordability can be combined: this is something people want to do for themselves, and do cheaply.

Pragmatism thrives on this demystification of architecture. Architectural courses around the

[2] HOUSE IN CAMBRIDGE, Massachusetts, USA, 2004. Uni-Architecture: Chaewon Kim

[3] HOUSE AND STUDIO LANG-KRÖLL, Gleissenberg, Germany, 2002. Florian Nagler Architekten

[4] SPARROW HOUSE, Lewes, UK, 2004. BBM Architects

[5] RURALZED, Devon, UK, 2005. Bill Dunster Architects

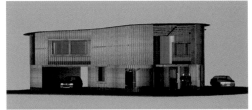

[6] FLEXI-LOG SYSTEM, 2004. Stuart Harris-Hancock

[7] THE PAPER HOUSE CONCEPT, 2004. Adriano Pupilli

[8] OPTIMA HOMES CONCEPT, 2004. Cartwright Pickard

world are recognizing the value of hands-on courses teaching practical architectural skills. These courses have necessarily low budgets and have led to a corresponding emphasis on design for the mass market, adapting and improving stock housing types by pooling knowledge and experience. The examples illustrated here, including the Design>Build>Texas project that operates out of Austin, Texas (see pp.180–3), illustrate a perennial concern of the pragmatic movement: low-cost, affordable housing that does not require complex new techniques of construction.

Ultimately, the relentless focus on the aesthetic of Modernism, and the emerging slickness in architectural photography, have sidelined innovation that is not immediately visible. Yet pragmatic architecture favours gradual improvement rather than a dramatic break with tradition. Mindful, perhaps, of political and social sensitivities to new building, sometimes a developed version of the vernacular acts as a useful means of enclosing an interior that is more innovative than it first appears; for example, both Mole Architects' Black House (see pp.198–201) and L'Atelier Provisoire's House at Castetner (see pp.142–5) use explicitly agricultural references, both visually and materially. Chaewon Kim's house in Cambridge, Massachusetts, makes a virtue of low-cost materials – translucent plastic, pre-rusted steel siding and composite wooden flooring [2] – as does Florian Nagler's House and Studio Lang-Kröll in Gleissenberg [3].

Materials innovation, including recycled and reclaimed materials, low-energy designs, making the most of tight plots, and restrictive planning legislation have all provided constraints and parameters from within which a new form of architecture is emerging. Sarah Wigglesworth's 'straw bale' house in London's Islington is a one-off, but it is also a project that spans an enormous amount of ground in both material innovation and aesthetic theory, taking as it does an effectively 'worthless' material such as straw and bringing it into the domestic realm (the material was also used in Hudson Architects' Cedar House in Norfolk, completed in 2005 [1]). The stripped-back, unadorned façade, be it wood, concrete or even metal, conveys a certain honesty.

Pragmatic architecture with an explicitly environmentally driven agenda is still relatively rare. Small projects such as Duncan Baker-Brown's Sparrow House [4] or Bill Dunster's RuralZed [5] are, for now, among the exceptions. Dunster has been explicit about the 'ordinariness' of his architecture – RuralZed is even described as 'the new ordinary', perhaps to mollify banks, which have demonstrated little affection for anything that deviates from convention. Dunster's ordinariness is a different kind of ordinary, but his point is that self-builders and local contractors alike should have no problems putting together one of his houses; they offer a very affordable solution. Much the same approach was promised by the so-called 'community architect' Walter Segal, whose cul-de-sac of houses in South London (now known as Walter's Way) was a celebrated community-led self-build project. This attitude is resurfacing in low-tech attempts to build with 'found' materials and prefabricated structures such as shipping containers, be it by large companies like Yorkon, a subsidiary of Portakabin, or by small studios searching for a breakthrough, such as architecture student Stuart Harris-Hancock with his Flexi-Log proposal [6], or the ultra-low-cost Paper House concept [7].[2] Even consumer-focused companies such as IKEA believe there is a market for prefabrication, and architects and manufacturers are collaborating to create new paradigms in housing [8, 9, 10].

The question remains as to whether to invest in these unproven new building technologies, or to focus on regenerating existing, albeit run-down, urban fabric. Can houses really be built for as little as £60,000 ($114,000) to solve the housing shortage, as demanded by the British government in 2005? And if so, will the resulting projects be 'pragmatic' from a design point of view or merely cheap, stripped-down versions of the benighted 'brick box'? Affordable housing is perhaps the most pressing concern facing many developed countries, and is a problem paid frequent lip service by theoretical schemes, student projects, ideas competitions and blue-sky thinking.

–

At the other extreme, what was formerly known as minimalism – actually expensive reductivism – is by no means dead. Arguably, there is a point at which minimalism and pragmatism coincide, from Mies van der Rohe, through contemporary works such as John Pawson's House in Germany of 2003 [12] or the Villa Nesselande by Hopman Architecten [11], to Jonathan Woolf's Brick Leaf House in London (see pp.192–5). While the material and tectonic approach demonstrated by these projects has a certain rough aestheticism, they are still undeniably expensive. Another factor to consider in relation to pragmatic architecture is variety; this is not a movement of easy classification. In the 1960s a new breed of architectural studio emerged, multi-disciplinary, media-aware and able to draw on the spirit and themes of emerging popular culture and fuse them with technological optimism and innovation. Debates about form and function were subverted by the desire for new architectural classifications – inflatable dwellings, portable buildings, 'fun palaces' and even cities that walk[3] – with candy-coloured interiors and overt, exaggerated symbolism.

The ascendance and brief dominance of post-Modern architecture in the 1980s and 1990s drew on the willingness for formal exploration and architectural narrative uncovered by the Pop era, and attracted strong criticism from die-hard progressives, who soon found themselves in the oxymoronic position of being seen as 'traditional' Modernists. A schism opened up, chronicled and widened by such books as Learning from Las Vegas, which set out the case for architecture to become an extension of existing media forms.[4] By the 1990s, many architecture studios were capable of synthesizing the views of both Venturi and Le Corbusier, merging them with the dizzying imagery and spontaneity of multi-media-based popular culture. Although fringe movements such as neo-classicism and minimalism defiantly refused to engage with this new cultural environment, suddenly post-Modernism's ability to 'quote' and reference was everywhere, and 'event architecture' superseded both Modernism and post-Modernism as the dominant architectural form, culminating in that most contemporary of building forms, the icon. Pragmatic architecture acknowledges our desire for symbolism, and the role that form and materials play in shaping our perception of home. Although the design commentators and taste-makers never abandoned Modernism, even once it shifted from harbinger of social revolution to urban pariah and thence to a fringe activity, favoured by enthusiasts, architects and combinations of the two, the conditions exist to encourage a panoply of stylistic and structural approaches: one size will no longer fit all.

[9] MODULAR2HOUSE, 2005. Studio 804, University of Kansas, School of Architecture and Urban Design

[10] PAD MODULAR HOMES, 2005. Pad – Michael Wallis

[11] VILLA NESSELANDE, Rotterdam, Netherlands, 2004. Hopman Architecten

1   Kent Kleinman and Leslie Van Duzer, 'Notes on Almost Nothing: Mies van der Rohe's Haus Lange and Haus Esters', *Newsline*, 02.01, Columbia University School of Planning and Preservation, New York.

2   www.thepaperhouse.net.

3   The London-based Archigram group (www.archigram.net) defined the generation, with outlandish, unbuildable proposals that merged science fiction with technological optimism.

4   Robert Venturi, Denise Scott Brown and Steven Izenour, *Learning from Las Vegas*, MIT Press, Cambridge MA, 1972.

[12] HOUSE IN GERMANY, 2003. John Pawson Architects

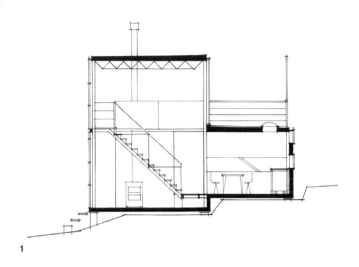

1

1   Section.

2   Ground-floor plan: [A] living room,
     [B] bedroom, [C] kitchen, [D] terrace.

3   The summer house is set deep in the woods,
     a translucent industrial box softened by its
     surroundings.

4   Night-time illumination reveals the scope of
     the glazing and opaque panels used in the
     construction.

5   The upper floor is half the size of the ground
     floor, creating space for a generous tree-top
     terrace.

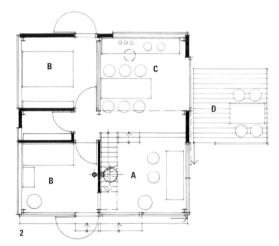

```
0          2.5m          5m
      7.5ft          15ft
```

2

The architect Peter Hesselgren
constructed this summer house
on the densely wooded island of
Kungshatt on Lake Mälaren, to the
west of Stockholm, for his own
personal use. Modest in scale and
ambition, the house nonetheless
makes use of standardized industrial
components to great effect. The
chief source of inspiration was the
famous postwar series of Case
Study houses, in particular Charles
and Ray Eames's celebrated Pacific
Palisades house of 1948, Case Study
number 8, which was famously
restructured at the last minute to
accommodate site conditions. The
summer house is similarly flexible in

form, drawing on the Swedish
tradition of maintaining a separate
summer house, merging it with the
themes of international Modernism.
    The architect describes the house
as a 'prototype of industrially
constructed summer living', and
Hesselgren built it with his artist
wife, Gunvor Larsson, over several
holidays from 2000 to 2004. The
design is developed from a 1989
project for a futuristic terrace house,
a project that Hesselgren developed
using steel structure and plywood
infill. The summer house also uses
a modular system, with a square
structural steel frame, 7 × 7.4
metres (23 × 24 feet), into which

panels have been fixed to form
rooms. The frame rests on nine
plinths, carefully sited on the edge of
the lake in the shade of several large
birch trees. Arranged within this
frame are six room 'modules' on two
floors, divided by partitions, sliding
glass doors and walls – there is no
central circulation space.
    The bedrooms are placed to the
east of the plan, two on the ground
floor and one on the upper storey.
Each bedroom has a low-placed
window, allowing the morning sun
to wake the occupants. On the first
floor is a broad south-west-facing
terrace running the full width of the
house, a space where the occupiers

3

4

5

KUNGSHATT
SUMMER HOUSE

Lake Mälaren, Sweden

2004

Peter Hesselgren and Gunvor Larsson

can be up in the tree canopy and catch the evening sun. A double-height multipurpose room at the northern corner of the cube contains the steel-and-wood open-tread staircase linking the two floors. A traditional stove heats the principal living space.

The exterior of the house is clad with specially treated plywood and the interior in Finnish birch. Finishes are left exposed throughout – steel ceiling trays, plywood and birch infill panels, and walls of translucent plastic in the bedrooms that combine privacy and light. Divested of the need to function as a day-to-day home, the ultra-compact footprint allows for minimal yet not minimalist living arrangements. Fixtures and fittings are chosen for pragmatic and emotive reasons.

The house has a bolted-together quality which respects the island's topography and flora, and celebrates the early Modernist optimism in the prefabricated house, built from off-the-shelf components that could be arranged in a variety of ways. Hesselgren is investigating the possibility of turning his 'industrial prototype' into a real product.

6

7

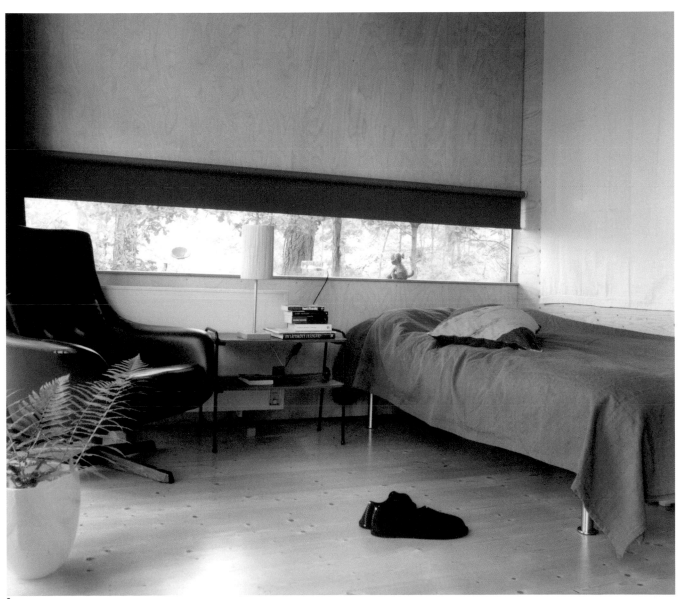

1 The street elevation, with its raised porch and large picture window to the kitchen.
2 Set on a long, slender site, the majority of the house is single-storey.

YALE BUILDING PROJECT

New Haven, Connecticut, USA

2004

Yale School of Architecture

1

2

Instituted in 1967, the Yale Building Project has so far completed 37 buildings, following the dictum that 'architecture cannot be learned without both an intellectual and a physical understanding of building as a discipline'. Every student in Yale's graduate school of architecture is required to participate. Over the decades the emphasis has evolved from broader community-centric projects into an exclusive focus on what the university describes as 'affordable, inner-city, single family dwellings'.

The 2004 Yale Building Project house is located on Hudson Street, over the road from the New Haven

Correctional Center. The adjacent site is abandoned, and the plot posed not only the challenge inherent in the Building Project – for novices to specify, detail and build a house – but in addition the need to maximize privacy while achieving the required accommodation. Six teams of ten people produced a series of designs for three-bedroom single family houses, which were reviewed by a jury that included members of the neighbourhood's housing services.

The chosen design is essentially a single-storey project, with a first-floor addition containing a bedroom and bathroom to the rear. The

3

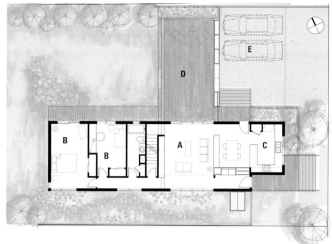

4

3 The shelving unit, cut by a computer-controlled saw, also forms the stair balustrade.

4 Ground-floor plan: [A] living room, [B] bedroom, [C] kitchen, [D] terrace, [E] garage/utility.

5 South elevation, illustrating the scissor-type roof.

6 North elevation.

5

6

building is long and narrow, with a kitchen at the street end, leading through a living area to two bedrooms at the quieter end. A staircase located in the middle leads to the master bedroom on the first floor. In side elevation, the house steps up to first-floor level by means of a long sloping roof, which also accommodates the 5.5-metre (18-foot) ceilings in the central living area. The scissor-type roof doubles back above the upstairs bedroom, providing a first-floor window facing east. There are generous external spaces, including a large deck extending from the sitting area and running along the north façade. A tall slatted screen separates the deck from the driveway, forming a private north-facing yard. A cedar-wood surround, 2.7 × 1.8 metres (9 × 6 feet) and 0.6 metres (2 feet) deep, frames the kitchen window, helping to distance occupants from the surroundings. The wall siding is painted blue, complementing the window surrounds.

The kitchen and living spaces are united in the same volume, separated only by the 2.4-metre (8-foot) dining bar and a double-sided storage wall that divides the kitchen from the entrance hall. Computerized Numerical Control technology was used to fabricate the complex staircase – joists and risers were constructed from 1.2 × 2.4 metre (4 × 8 foot) plywood sheets, milled so that they extended outwards and upwards from the staircase to form an 'egg-crate' shelving system, the face of which is a gently undulating surface. Larger openings are included to hold a television set and ornaments.

The 2004 house is a stretched version of the suburban archetype, with carefully thought-out details to maximize affordability without compromising on the key architectonic elements that give the house its character. In common with the 2002 and 2003 houses, mono-pitched wooden frame structures that occupied similar suburban sites, the 2004 Yale Building Project was not about an abstract, intellectual architecture, but rather a low-cost project for the common good.

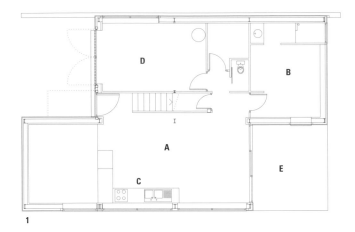

1 Ground-floor plan: [A] living room,
[B] bedroom, [C] kitchen, [D] studio,
[E] terrace.

2 The house sits atop a concrete slab, detailed
like a functional farm building.

3 The corrugated siding and three different roof
pitches create an abstract, industrial profile.

4 The structure also mimicks the house-and-
lean-to configuration of so many rural
dwellings.

0   2.5m   5m
    7.5ft   15ft

HOUSE AT CASTETNER (MAISON THIERRY ET CORINNE)

Pyrénées-Atlantiques, France

2003

L'Atelier Provisoire

The Maison Thierry et Corinne is a modest structure in a small village on the outskirts of Orthez, in France's Pyrénées-Atlantiques region. Any coherent local vernacular has long since disappeared, as traditional Béarnais-style farmhouses and rural housing are joined by new, ersatz bungalows and cottages, built by city-dwellers escaping the sprawl emerging from the north.

The house attempts to bridge this aesthetic divide, mixing the hard-edged style of the modern working agricultural building with compact dimensions and a very domestic feel – this is a family home for a young couple with two daughters. Having

looked for a house in the area without success, they decided to build their own after being introduced to the architects, Bordeaux-based L'Atelier Provisoire, via mutual friends. The result is a house of metal: the frame, walls and ceiling are all steel, with corrugated siding and roofing giving it a distinctive visual quality. Yet rather than build big open-plan spaces, the house is planned in a conventional sense; it was more interesting, the studio speculated, to build a domestic-type structure with an industrial material rather than a hangar.

By combining two different types of roof construction, pitch and pent,

the house presents itself as a brooding silhouette on the horizon, a modern update of the stand-alone farmhouse with a classic lean-to, whether for cattle or living space. Echoes of a nearby stone barn can be seen in the angle of the roofs, although from a distance the brown-coloured metal fragments and dissolves the various planes into a brooding superstructure, creating a confusingly obtuse structure sitting atop a light-coloured concrete plinth. The house is located in the centre of a long, thin, sloping plot, set back from the road and oriented north–south. Inside, dimensions are compact, just 130 square metres

5 A large kitchen/dining area occupies the 'lean-to'. A tiled floor runs throughout.

6 South elevation.

7 North elevation, with French doors to the kitchen/diner at left.

6

7

(1400 square feet), and fixtures and fittings are unpretentious. The accommodation is limited to just two main rooms on each floor in addition to the large kitchen/living area, the heart of the house that is located beneath the 'lean-to'. Here the interior roof is raised up to the eaves; the floor is polished slate throughout, and a wooden staircase ascends in the centre of the plan, beneath the intersection of the two roof types. A strip of steel windows above the kitchen counter frames a view of the landscape and the inside/outside division is further enhanced by the French doors that open directly into the field. Upstairs is a bathroom, two small children's rooms and a tiny office space, while the master bedroom is downstairs, along with a small studio.

This house certainly does not conform to any agrarian fantasies – this remote part of south-western France is subject to the same technological and social pressures as any other part of Europe. Yet the Maison Thierry et Corinne has established itself as something of a local landmark – 'the sheet-metal house' – and represents a small victory for striking, low-cost, practical rural design.

1 View from garden – Marsh View is the radical reconstruction of an existing bungalow, extended to form a home and studio.

2 A concrete ramp rises up to the entrance, at left. The small entrance hall doubles up as a dye room.

3 The towering brick chimney on the west façade, shown shortly after completion, gives the main room a lofty ceiling, at the top of which is a skylight.

1

2

Marsh View is a house that will grow into its landscape, a small family home with an unconventional exterior, a generous interior and an extensive use of vernacular materials that identify the building with its Norfolk surroundings. It occupies the site of a bungalow with few, if any, redeeming features. This was demolished, retaining the south and east walls as the basis of the new-build. Despite its respect for vernacular traditions, planning permission in this designated area of outstanding natural beauty was granted only on appeal.

Lynch's client, Alison Mitchell, a weaver, wanted a weekend retreat.

They discussed the idea of a residence that would be a series of spaces and views rather than a set of conventional rooms. Mitchell wanted 'a tall section of roofing with a skylight at the top so the full moon would cast shadows into this high-up void', and Lynch responded by creating a 7.5-metre (25-foot) chimney stack as the house's pivotal feature. This stark brick chimney is met by two painted softwood-clad walls, the roof sloping steeply up to the corner. From the adjacent water meadows the chimney is like a tower, a man-made feature punctuating this flat landscape just like the nearby church spire and

timber mill. This elevation shields a south-facing courtyard, accessed by broad sliding glass doors from the living room. Two ponds have been dug: the 'evening pond', at the edge of the site, and the 'morning pond', nestling in the angle of the Z-shaped floor plan by the front entrance.

Inside, the main space is towering, as Mitchell requested, with a wedgelike rooflight, an oculus soaking the room in daylight and creating a place to watch the stars at night. From the entrance-cum-dye-room at the southern end of the property, one enters a kitchen and dining area, which leads to a study and the inside/outside space created

MARSH VIEW HOUSE

Norfolk, UK

2003

Lynch Architects

4

4   The living room rises steeply to the oculus in the northern corner of the building.

5   Daylight floods in, illuminating the fireplace in the corner.

6   While the exterior is black-painted softwood planks, the interior is lined with plywood, with a concrete floor throughout.

7   Section through studio room.

8   Ground-floor plan: [A] living room, [B] bedroom, [C] kitchen, [D] studio, [E] terrace.

5   **6**

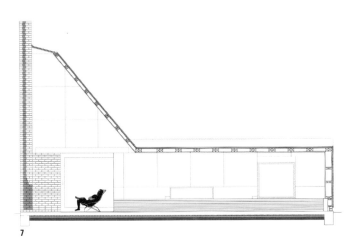

7

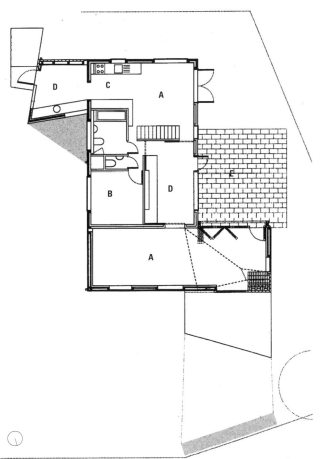

8

by re-using the existing terrace. On the first floor are two bedrooms, although there are sleeping arrangements for eight in total.

Natural lighting is gathered from as many points as possible, including rooflights and corner windows, with no central mullions. The internal cladding is plywood, as is the structural skin, an economical way of creating the large parabolic roof. Rooms are divided by full-height sliding plywood doors, hung from ceiling-mounted tracks. The external brickwork is blackened, in a nod to local vernacular. The aesthetic was not a sop to the planning process, but stemmed from a genuine fascination with the roughness of the construction process, the sense of an unfinished object, constantly weathering, a toughness of spirit that addresses both landscape and ideas of the home. Marsh View is far from contemporary views of innovative architecture: it uses tried and tested technology, with experimentation dedicated to reducing costs. It is not focused only on traditional materials, but on an almost unfashionable notion of domesticity that places the hearth at the centre of the home. It is unique yet familiar, a building established to continue an ongoing narrative.

1

2

HOUSE IN AGGSTALL

Freising, Upper Bavaria, Germany

2000

Hild und K Architekten

Throughout the greater part of the twentieth century, few Modernist architecture studios combined strict commitment to function with decorative elements; frills were not just aesthetically disdained, they were ideologically rejected. Today ideology has been usurped by fashion, architecture references faster-moving consumerism, and housing design increasingly follows the pattern set out by high-end consumer items. One feature that distinguishes one mass-market product from another is ornament, whether in the form of distinctive colour palettes, materials, or applied pattern and decoration. At the

volume end of the housing market, ornament has always been present, whether in decorative brickwork or plasterwork, or in interior finishes and fittings. But at the bespoke, architect-designed end – a tiny percentage of new-builds – ornament is usually conspicuous by its absence: the legacy of Modernism dies hard.

Andreas Hild and Dionys Ottl form the Munich firm of Hild und K. Their portfolio is eclectic – car-parks, warehouses, private homes and performance spaces. Ornament is a theme that runs throughout. They state boldly that they 'don't believe in the style called Modernism … it's

possible to select the architecture according to the needs or message of the project'.

At first glimpse, this private house in Aggstall, about 50 kilometres (30 miles) south-east of Ingolstadt, does not appear especially unusual. It is pragmatic, a brick-built, apparently traditionalist structure, which blends seamlessly into the local vernacular. On closer inspection, unusual elements reveal themselves. The most radical departure is the relief-patterned brick walls, painted cream and laid in a deep-set diamond pattern. This gives the walls a fuzzy quality from a distance but a more traditional solidity up close. In the

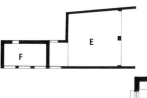

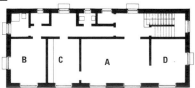

3

4

1 The new house presents an ostensibly conventional face to the world, its façades neat and ordered and the roof gently pitched.
2 Up close, the decorative brickwork becomes apparent.
3 Ground-floor plan: [A] living room, [B] bedroom, [C] kitchen, [D] studio, [E] garage/utility, [F] orangery.
4 Details are reductivist, such as the handrail incorporated within the stair balustrade.
5 The dining room: plain white walls and wooden floors are used throughout. The double doors open on to the garden.

evening, long shadows are cast into the deep patterns, making the surface appear almost diaphanous, an effect the architects call 'playful surfacing'. Hild describes this as an 'architectonic' solution, part of an attempt to make the house a paradox – 'hyper-normal' and irregular, yet buildable. Above all, it is about originality, a reinterpretation of the traditional but run-down property previously on the site.

The measurements of the pre-existing house provided constraints, as the planning authority insisted that heights and site dimensions were matched. The new house is topped off by an asymmetric pitched

roof, using recycled tiles for an aged effect. The main façade comprises an ordered series of five floor-to-ceiling windows, the middle three below a centrally placed portico, with five evenly spaced oak-framed windows on the first floor. Inside, the plan is simplicity itself, a traditional arrangement with rooms accessed from a main corridor. Internal finishes include oak flooring, white plaster walls and an unselfconscious absence of mouldings and cornicing.

The design's proportions recall the functional Classicism of the pavilions in Claude-Nicholas Ledoux's 'ideal city' of Chaux

or Aldo Rossi's early villas. This 'hyper-normality' is fundamental to Hild und K's work, stemming from admiration of the vernacular, and their pragmatic, DIY approach. It is a rejection of the high-style, vision-over-substance approach, yet does not eschew the rigorous attention to detail and materials that characterizes high quality design.

5

THE BOX HOUSE

New South Wales, Australia

1999

Neeson Murcutt Architects

2

The Box House is a first project, a prototypical object designed without sight of the surrounding landscape, into which it was then dropped. In one respect, the Box House is representative of the Australian 'shack' tradition, that very pragmatic means of making shelter that responds to the extremes of the Antipodean climate, the harshness of the terrain, the undeniable sense of space and the use and reuse of simple building materials such as corrugated iron, wood and concrete.

Located on the New South Wales coast, some six hours from Sydney, the Box House is a 6.3-metre (21-foot) cube, raised up on concrete supports. A square wooden deck is offset from the main plan, in the manner of Kasimir Malevich's suprematist compositions, providing an external eating and living area and space for one of two access ramps that descend to the grassy plains surrounding the building. An external circular metal watertank stands atop an open framework at the rear of the site, its ribbed sides drawing inevitable comparisons with the work of Nick Murcutt's father, the architect Glenn Murcutt, with whom he shares a clear empathy in the way in which he accentuates the physical intensity of a simple object adrift in the landscape.

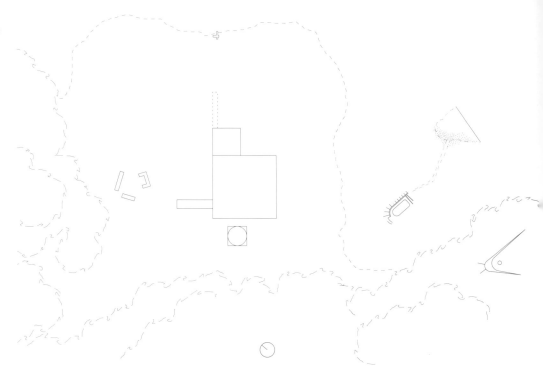

3

While Murcutt Senior's houses stand defiantly apart from nature in form and materials, the Box House is basic, a holiday home that can do away with the creature comforts associated with a year-round residence. Yet despite the external cast-iron bath (heated by a fire) and pit toilet, the house feels far from oppressively austere, and the feeling of being encased in wood and glass, illuminated by candles, surrounded by furnishings that eschew the clichéd Modernist canon, is without doubt domestic and familiar. Construction methods are tried and tested – a wooden-framed box built from local hardwood by a local contractor – but what sets this particular shack apart from its archetype is the exquisite detailing and proportions. Windows are set flush with the wooden sides, including the two large glass openings above the double-height living area. The bed deck is raised upon a mezzanine above, reached via a ladder, and shuttered openings both frame the views and animate the façades.

The total budget was just a fraction of the sums expended on Murcutt and Neeson's later, more polished works. The absence of plumbing and electricity helps to explain the low cost, and also accentuates the Box House's prototypical status – this is an object that could easily be replicated, honed and improved, a model space for a simpler life.

4

HOUSE IN WANDLITZ

Berlin, Germany

2003

Heide von Beckerath Alberts Architekten

Heide von Beckerath Alberts's house for a young married couple has an idyllic suburban location in Wandlitz, a lakeside community on the edge of the Bernau Forest, about 20 kilometres (12 miles) north of Berlin. Wandlitz, favoured by members of the East German Politburo, is an ideal suburb constructed along such rigorous lines that initial American spy satellite images led analysts to believe that a military facility was being laid out. The communist residential ideal was a combination of Soviet dacha and Levittown, complete with communal facilities and generous three-storey houses, surrounded by a sizeable wall.

This house is located in a new part of the community, which now houses overspill from Berlin. The area maintains strict zoning and planning laws, dictating materials, colours and the angle of the pitch of roofs. As a result, the Wandlitz house initially appears highly conventional. Yet look again, and familiarity dissolves into the uncanny. There is something self-consciously different about the structure, like the mock houses constructed on military ranges for target practice or to cover up entrances to military bunkers, an effect heightened by the ladder rungs on the large chimney. This is

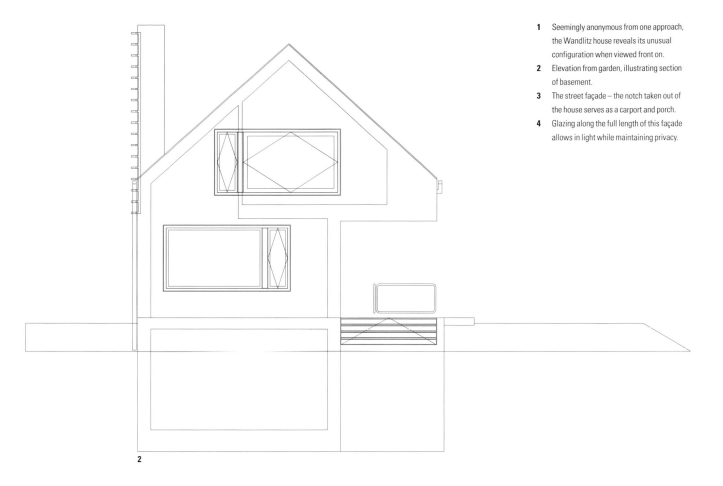

1 Seemingly anonymous from one approach, the Wandlitz house reveals its unusual configuration when viewed front on.
2 Elevation from garden, illustrating section of basement.
3 The street façade – the notch taken out of the house serves as a carport and porch.
4 Glazing along the full length of this façade allows in light while maintaining privacy.

2

3

4

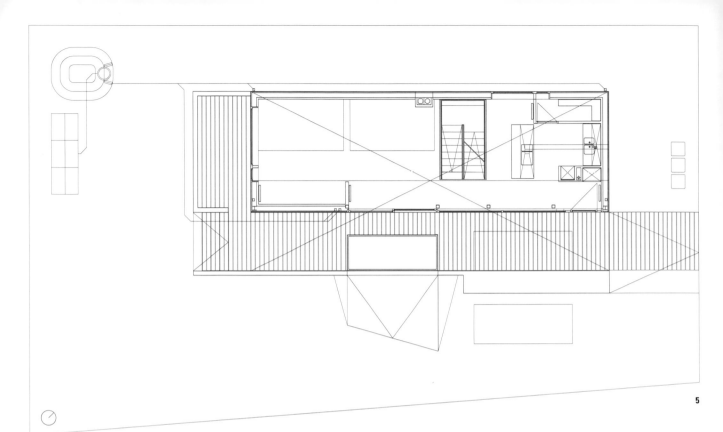

5

a suburban house with a twist. The community ruled that only one-storey, pitched-roof bungalows be constructed, yet the Wandlitz House squeezes three levels into its volume by the construction of a large basement (much like the original Politburo homes).

The ground floor features a large cut-out, giving the house its distinctive section and providing a car-parking space, a deck, and a window sunk below ground bringing daylight into the basement. The ground-floor façade has floor-to-ceiling glass, with privacy provided by diaphanous curtains. The basement contains a storage area,

a bathroom, a guest room with open fireplace, and a small external courtyard. On the ground floor is the kitchen and living area, with a double-height space extending into the eaves. The second floor contains two bedrooms, each with a door into the linear bathroom.

The basement is formed from slabs of reinforced concrete, a firm foundation for the house, built around a combination of steel framing and structural wood. Walls are panelled and plastered, with the first-floor slab also built from wood. The staircase has steel treads and a combination of open mesh and wooden panels as balustrading,

a simple zigzagging form taking up little space. Inside walls and finishes are white, offsetting the warm stone floor and sisal mats. Roofing tiles are grey, as is the external rendering, with grey-framed steel windows set into the austere façade.

Initially the house stood alone, surrounded by scrubby vegetation; it has been joined by new houses as plots are sold. That traditional symbol of suburban isolation, the hedge, has been planted to preserve privacy. The design gently subverts traditional forms, but uses hard-wearing industrial materials and careful planning to make a welcoming home.

5 Plan of ground-floor living area showing extent of first floor above car port.
6 The ground floor, viewed from the kitchen, with the window wall at left.
7 Looking from the ground-floor living room to towards the kitchen and the staircase constructed from lengths of folded steel.

1

2

MAISON DEJARDIN-HENDRICÉ

Comblain-au-Pont, Belgium

2004

Atelier d'Architecture Pierre Hebbelinck

This three-bedroom house is located on the south slope of the Ourthe Valley, near the Belgian village of Comblain-au-Pont, on the site of an ancient Gallo-Roman cemetery. The site is raised 4 metres (13 feet) above street level, and the new house is set on this 'peak', above a gully formed from the path cut into the ground leading up to the entrance.

Externally, the project resembles a perfect cube, formed from four structural elements of Cor-ten steel, welded together off-site then transported and assembled on a single day. This coming together of components followed 30 months of research, during which the project's evolution was tracked in detail (and catalogued in an accompanying book, sheathed in its own steel dust-jacket). The clients are a young family, and the budget was low. The ambitious design was accepted on condition that the design and construction process was carefully monitored, and that a prefabrication system be devised to keep costs down. Helpfully, M. Dejardin is a director of a company manufacturing industrial boilers, thereby giving access to technical expertise in putting together large-scale metalwork. The basic concept is that the steel cube rests atop the supporting blockwork, set into the ground. The pathway doubled as access for lorries, and left space for a carport and entrance hall once the project was finished.

Hebbelinck has used naval technology for the cube's structure, coupled with techniques used for large-scale heating installations. As well as its obvious structural properties, Cor-ten steel is intended gradually to oxidize, and the surface will slowly weather to a dark brown, with hints of purple and orange. The final hue is intended to resemble the village's stonework.

Dimensions were dictated by cost and construction limits with elements sized according to the maximum

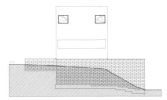

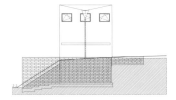

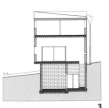

3

4

5

1-2 The entrance is cut into the slope of the site and screened by two large concrete slabs. The first floor is then craned into place.

3 Site elevations and section: a box atop a concrete raft.

4-5 The prefabricated steel box forming the second storey is positioned, leaving a cube offset above the entrance.

6 The finished house is a perfect cube, created from Cor-ten steel which gradually rusts to a rich red patina.

dimensions allowed on the road from factory to site. The attention to detail even extended to the manufacture of a 3-metre (10-foot) prototype. Once final sizes had been established, internal spaces were developed to emphasize a human scale, bringing this rather sculptural object (the hulks of rusted steel bring American artist Richard Serra to mind) into the domestic realm.

Steel was hailed as a revolutionary house-building material in the interwar and postwar period. Spurred on by such high-profile projects as the Case Study houses in California, the steel frame was deemed the most cost-efficient way of defining a space, providing an adaptable basis for the open-plan style and a sound structural frame for dramatic statements of intent such as cantilevers and glass curtain walls. The Dejardin-Hendricé house is different: the four steel sections are not just frames, they are clad frames – self-contained structures that eschew the lightweight nature of standard prefabricated building in favour of a more experimental approach. The architect's stated intention was to further research into housing technology in Belgium, bringing other contractors and economic factors into play.

6

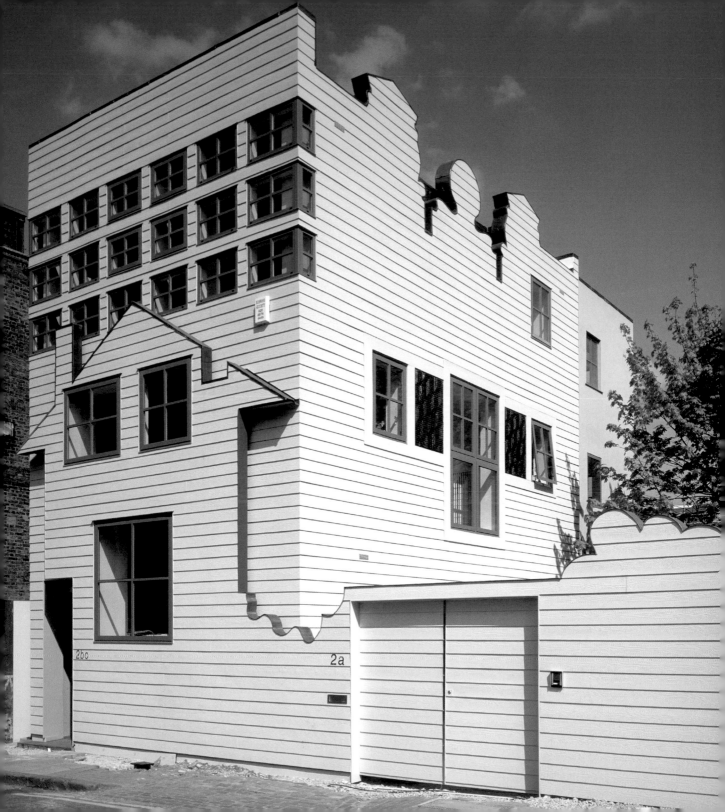

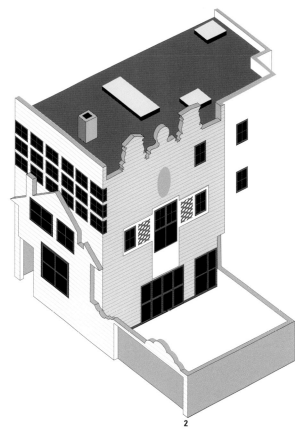

2

BLUE HOUSE

London, UK

2002

FAT (fashion architecture taste)

As the 'mother of all arts', architecture is unapologetically highbrow. Humour is a rare commodity in the profession, which tends, in the main, towards taking itself rather seriously. Happily, not all architects are content to adhere to establishment tastes. The Blue House, in the East End of London, is the family home of Sean Griffiths, one of the directors of FAT (fashion, architecture, taste), a deliberately iconoclastic practice that engages with everything from exhibition design to mass housing, and from healthcare to car parks.

Ostensibly a conventional three-storey terrace house, with an open-plan ground floor and bedrooms above, the Blue House delights in visual games, offering up four apparently conflicting stylistic references within the space of two elevations. The façade, painted powder-blue, is clad in hard-wearing cementitious siding, a mixture of cement, sand and cellulose fibre that is impervious to moisture and decay. In skilled hands, this is a flexible material that can be cut and shaped like timber boarding, and Griffiths has ensured that it makes maximum stylistic impact. The street entrance is framed by an extruded representation of the classic house form: three windows, door and pitched roof with chimney, rendered

in a deliberately childlike fashion. To the right, the step-forward dissolves into a wavy line of fencing – a hedge? – before it resolves itself as the garage door and then bubbles up, cloudlike, beyond. Above the front door is a grid of 18 small windows, mimicking the façade of an office building and creating a miniature cityscape, a place of both work and play, explicitly evoking the themes that underpin the regeneration of this part of London. The garden façade is topped with abstracted Dutch gables, returning a decorative roofscape to an area that has been gradually stripped of historical detail and visual interest.

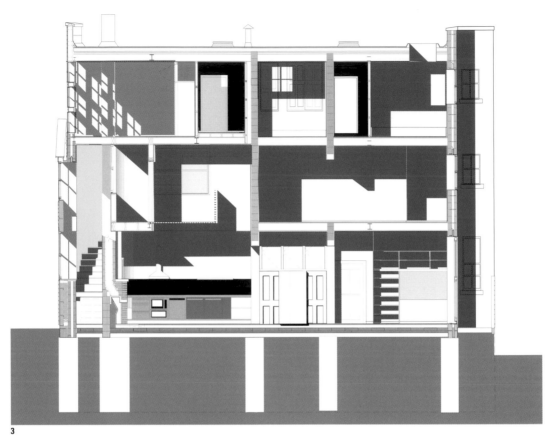

3

4

The floor plan is set back from the main façade to create circulation space, and the staircases curve in an agreeably idiosyncratic fashion. The internal spaces use contrasting colours and decorative touches that have long since been dismissed as kitsch, such as polished parquet flooring and wooden balustrades with hearts cut into them. The 18 small windows illuminate the master bedroom, while pink stairs lead to a child's room. The decked garden, accessed via a broad sweep of folding windows in the kitchen, contains a traditional garden shed, a clear, if tongue-in-cheek, aesthetic antecedent for the house.

All too often, architects' own houses are elegant yet unconvincing, carefully presented as examples of perfection rather than individual character: for an architect to build his or her own house is a very public statement of private taste. The Blue House defiantly bucks that trend; if it showcases anything, it is perhaps the belief that blind adherence to the strictures of taste is not a healthy way to live.

3 Section through the house: the layout is ostensibly conventional, but maximizes space by pushing the stair to the edge of the plans and incorporates double-height spaces.

4 The 'cloud' feature in the front wall, behind which lies the garden shed, with the decorative mansard beyond.

5 The kitchen/dining area opens up to the garden to the side of the house.

6 The master bedroom is located behind the 18 small windows that make up the upper level of the front façade.

5

6

1

SUMMER HOUSE

Åland, Finland

2002

Todd Saunders and Tommie Wilhelmsen

This modest Finnish villa was designed by Canadian Todd Saunders and Norwegian Tommie Wilhelmsen. It is located on a small wooded island in the Åland archipelago, the front door just a few metres from the Baltic Sea. Saunders and Wilhelmsen both teach at Norway's Bergen School of Architecture, and the process of building the house was hugely instructive for the architects and for the students who worked on the project, with Mats Odin Røstøy and three others acting as carpenters and key contractors.

The 42 square metre (450 square foot) property, an occasional summer house, makes the most of its idyllic location, and the architects have endeavoured to make the design environmentally responsible. The structure is created almost entirely from timber, insulation is provided by woven linseed fibres, and linseed oil was used to treat and weatherproof the timber. All wood comes from a local sawmill, and the house is raised on short pillars, allowing the building to sit lightly upon its site, protecting existing tree roots and stumps on the forest floor.

The Summer House is arranged as a long wooden structure, a strip of wood 'folded', with eight right-angled corners forming four distinct elements: two sleeping areas with central bathroom, a terrace, a living-room and access to a first-floor roof deck. The folded structure therefore forms floors, walls, ceilings and decks, keeping the basic components of the house to a minimum for a client with a slender budget. The design also allows the living spaces to be opened up into one large area, with sliding glass doors throughout.

The small footprint posed challenges to maximize the available floor plan, and the Summer House is arranged as a series of multi-function spaces. 'One can eat breakfast in the morning sun on the terrace,' say the architects; '20 people can sit along

1   Set on wooded islands in the Åland
    archipelago, the house is woven between
    existing trees.

2   Slats allow in sun and provide privacy – the
    upper floor terrace is reached via an external
    staircase.

3   Plan and section: [A] living room,
    [B] bedroom.

2

the front of the cabin watching the evening sun, eat dinner outside on the [terrace outside] the bedroom … [and] open all the glass doors to form one space for larger groups of people.' It is, in their words, 'a house without borders'.

Although such freedom is drawn from Modernism's embrace of the free-flowing plan and the social benefits of 'open-plan living', the Summer House's compact footprint would barely make a dent on the floor areas of many sprawling Modernist houses. Instead, its aesthetic and formal rationales are subsumed by a desire for flexibility. Having existed for more than eight

decades, 'Modernism' has ultimately evolved into just another choice. The Summer House belongs to an organic tradition, growing out of the small-scale domestic vernacular and laying claim to be a stylistic continuation, rather than a sharp break with the past. It may be an 'iconic object', but the design is not so concerned with contrasting forms and materials with its setting, choosing instead slowly to weather and blend in with its surroundings. It represents a less orthodox and dictatorial modernism.

3

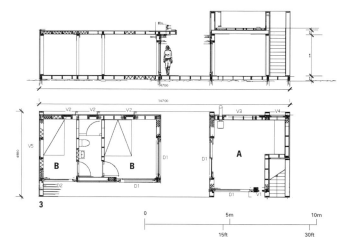

MUKAROV HOUSE

Prague, Czech Republic

1996–2000

Ivan Kroupa with Radka Kurcíková

The Mukarov House and its partner, the Minimal House, occupy a wooded site to the east of Prague. The main house has a small footprint, allowing it to slot among mature trees, and rises up to a fourth-floor studio overlooking the site. The north and south façades have no windows, protecting the interior against the harsh climate and from being overlooked. The other two façades are extensively glazed, with views across the tree tops and the forest to the east and west. The planting acts as a natural sunblind, with the tulip tree in front of the east façade helpfully shedding its leaves in winter to allow sunlight in.

The stair void runs through all four storeys, with views to the rooflight above. As one ascends to the top-floor studio, the natural light becomes stronger and stronger. Kroupa and Kurcíková have determined that individual residential functions for each floor are user-defined, with a series of movable walls and curtains to create privacy as needed. The key uses, such as living, sleeping and bathing, are incorporated along the edges of the plan, leaving the maximum amount of free floor space. The architects are open to the possibility of future changes in 'function, surfaces, colours and furniture'; even to 'possible extensions with different geometry and lighter material'.

If the Mukarov House is a paean to flexibility, then its sister structure, the Minimal House, is an object lesson in spontaneity: it was merely 'a few minutes from the intention to the concept, a few weeks from the concept to the completed building', according to Kurcíková. A 'transparent wooden tunnel', the single-storey structure is set among mature trees in the grounds of the main house – 'not a house surrounded by a garden, but a garden with a house'. The building is a folded structure, which wraps around on three sides, oversailing

1

2

1, 3 The garden studio building – the Minimal House – was a later addition, designed to be swiftly integrated by the rampaging plants.

2 The garden building features an integral pivoting wall that can turn the space from studio into guest accommodation.

3

4   The Mukarov House contains a large top-floor studio with a mezzanine set in a double-height space.

5   Floor plans of the Mukarov House: [A] living space, [B] bedroom, [C] kitchen, [D] study, [E] utility, [F] terrace, [G] roof terrace.

6   Section through the Mukarov House.

7   The Mukarov House is finished in basic, economical materials, such as this oriented strand-board stair to the studio space.

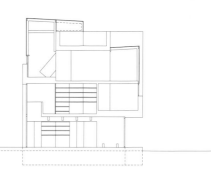

6

the enclosed structure to create an integral deck. The roof is clad in metal and folds down to form the northern façade. Climbing plants colonize the façade, and a vine grows through a slot in the timber floor and roof.

Inside the pavilion, walls, floors and ceiling are all clad in wood. The main space can be subdivided by a giant pivoting partition, which can be folded back to open it up or swung across to create smaller rooms. This allows for various layouts, depending on use. The pavilion has been a private house and an architecture studio, and is now a painting studio. The architects expect it to return to residential occupation in years to come.

The two structures complement each other, and are low-cost, contemporary usages of two architectural archetypes, the garden pavilion and the single family house. They make extensive use of unfinished construction materials, such as raw rendered partitions and staircases formed from cut panels of OSB (oriented strand board) in the main house, to create a stripped-back, basic aesthetic.

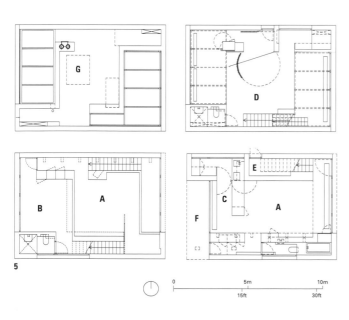

5

0   5m   10m
15ft   30ft

7

COURTYARD HOUSES

Matosinhos, Portugal

1999

Souto Moura Arquitectos

The Portugese architect Eduardo Souto de Moura is known for his serene approach to architecture, reducing elements to their bare essentials without compromising functionality. These nine new houses were built in the former vegetable garden of an old villa. The garden had been divided up into parcels of land, cut across by a new road, leaving one triangle-shaped parcel of land with space for a single house, and a larger trapezium-shaped parcel of land of approximately 7340 square metres (1.8 acres). Souto de Moura's proposal fills the larger plot with four small houses and five larger ones.

The plots are filled to their full extent, with each of the nine single-storey houses pared back to geometric and architectural essentials, parallel walls supporting three 'strips' of concrete for the roofs. Between the walls is a series of courtyard gardens, with the intention that vegetation will eventually reclaim the bare rendering and merge the houses with the surrounding landscape. The essential elements of shelter – walls and ceilings – are simplified, little more than a contemporary update of the prehistoric dolmen.

Souto de Moura's houses, like their vernacular predecessors, combine architectonic spaces with the practical need for sun-shading and the ability to have outdoor 'rooms'. Each of these single-storey houses is arranged around a series of courtyards, providing internal vistas and a self-contained landscape. These are not small properties – the larger houses have four bedrooms – and the linear plots allow a generous spatial arrangement. The white-rendered walls lend a simplicity that speaks of function and pragmatism, rather than a neurotic fear of clutter. There is, in fact, clutter visible here, for example in the necessary accumulation of rooftop extracts and flues, or in the juxtaposition of

2

1 A typical house in the development, viewed
   from its high-walled garden and (empty)
   swimming pool in the foreground.

2 From the house, each garden seems like an
   extension of the living space. The large
   glazed walls are kept as free from obstruction
   as possible.

material and texture where rendered wall meets stone and flagstone.

Minimalism's detractors point to its essentially sybaritic nature and the paradox at its heart – that in order to appear to consume less, an architectural process of necessary complexity (and expense) needs to be undertaken. In contrast, reductivist architecture shares few of minimalism's foibles, and starts to look even more practical in the hot, arid Mediterranean landscape. It is here that the much-vaunted fusion of inside/outside space can be explored, unbound by environmental constrictions and the vagaries of the northern European climate. In these

houses, the response to the site is undeniably architectural, but the thrust of the project comes from the proportional sophistication rather than a reliance on visual simplicity. This is a characteristic of Souto de Moura's work, and indicative of his interest in minimalist art, but it is also an explicit acknowledgement that housing forms are enduring rather than ephemeral.

3

4

5

3   A view looking out across the development.

4-5 From the outside, the detailing is almost
        brutally barren.

6   Floor plan of a typical house: [A] living room,
        [B] bedroom, [C] kitchen, [D] studio,
        [E] garage/utility, [F] swimming pool,
        [G] courtyard.

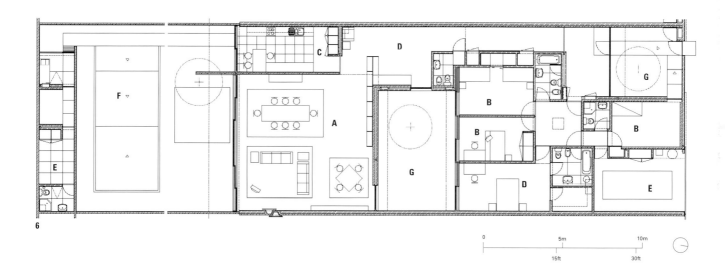

6

0   5m   10m

15ft   30ft

1-2 Section drawings: [A] living room,
[B] bedroom, [C] kitchen, [D] dining room,
[E] cellar.

3 The garden façade, with its skewed geometry
and extensive use of unpainted timber.

4 The garden and house beyond, showing the
deliberately expressionist angles.

MAISON MALICE

Brussels, Belgium

2001

Jean Leclercq

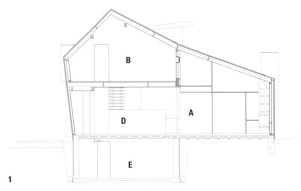

1

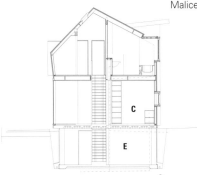

2

In Belgium, official housing policy has traditionally encouraged home ownership over rental – the constitution states that citizens have a right to a 'dignified life', and the private house has become an integral element of this right. The country benefits from low land prices and a proliferation of private development plots. As a result, free-standing single family houses are widespread, an endless suburbia that covers a far higher proportion of land than in other European nations. Suburban living has, as elsewhere, become clichéd shorthand for stultifying convention. The Maison Malice is an architectural response

to the cliché, a family home that gently subverts the status quo and improves the quality of life. Located in a typical suburb, on a typical plot, Jean Leclercq's house is clad in wood and shingle, a relatively conventional exterior that has been given a twist by the skewed geometry of the external walls, with roof and walls wrapping themselves around the building's core. Conventional elements, such as a garage and chimney stack, are also affected by this mild expressionism.

The site is densely wooded, and the four-bedroom family house makes the most of the existing vegetation through its

unconventional orientation: the house divides the plot lengthways, creating a garden for the morning and one for the evening. The extensive use of decking and floor-to-ceiling glazing brings the outside in, a cliché of Modernist design, but an arrangement that the suburban archetype usually ignores. Inside, the L-shaped floor plan emphasizes the importance of the family unit. Living areas are divided by generous circulation spaces which provide a distinct division between public and private and views across and through the space.

Jean Leclercq has kept the detailing deliberately simple and

3

4

5

6

7

8

pure. Internal finishes are naked wood, and for the most part walls are white, with the occasional splash of bold colour such as bright yellow in the master bedroom. All storage and function are relegated to one elevation, allowing the other façades to be largely composed of glass.

What animates the spaces is not complex detail but light and the facility for activity. The double-height reception reveals a garden façade that is almost entirely glazed, the treated wood frames pushed right to the edges of the building envelope. The room is generous but austere, with a fireplace faced with two sheets of plywood and a stainless-

steel flue disappearing up through the roof. Elsewhere, there is an absence of mouldings and decoration; the open-tread staircase is unpainted Douglas fir; and the overall feeling is childlike and free, ascetic rather than minimal, unconfined by domestic tradition and adult convention.

In the suburban context, when houses are so often closed and confined, their contents famously impossible to read or divine, the Maison Malice is a revelation. Without jeopardizing privacy or the trappings of ownership, this house has transformed traditional space into a place of possibility.

DESIGN >BUILD >TEXAS

Johnson City, Texas, USA

2004

University of Texas at Austin, School of Architecture

Design>Build>Texas is a design/build studio for upper-level architecture students at the School of Architecture at the University of Texas at Austin. The intention behind the module, led by Louise Harpman, a professor in the school, and Russell Krepart, a junior faculty member and master carpenter, was to create an educational prototype that also resulted in a building prototype. Although the result is far removed from the conventional suburban home or élitist Modernist villa, it offers an alternative 'first home' solution to first-time buyers being courted by an aggressively developer-led market.

The 18-strong team designed the house using several key factors, notably the available time and budget and the nature of the site. The landscape was crucial. The site, on a 390-hectare (960-acre) ranch outside Johnson City, west of Austin, was donated by a sponsor who also contributed to the cost of building. Texas Hill Country, as the area is known, has fragile, shallow topsoil and unpredictable rainfall. The plot's remoteness contrasts with the sprawl slowly engulfing nearby Johnson City, making for a more considered design process.

The house is arranged as two separate rectangular pavilions, one

for living, one for sleeping, unified by a mono-pitched roof and broad porch, all on a concrete slab. A covered carport provides additional shelter and storage. The aesthetic is reminiscent of local ranch housing, although such structures are typically more ad hoc and pragmatic than this finely honed design. Like ranch housing, though, the project is arranged as a series of components, rather than one unit, and uses a construction module of 2.4 × 6 metres (8 × 20 feet) to allow adaptation to a prefabricated construction process. Other aspects of local agricultural building influenced the design, such as the

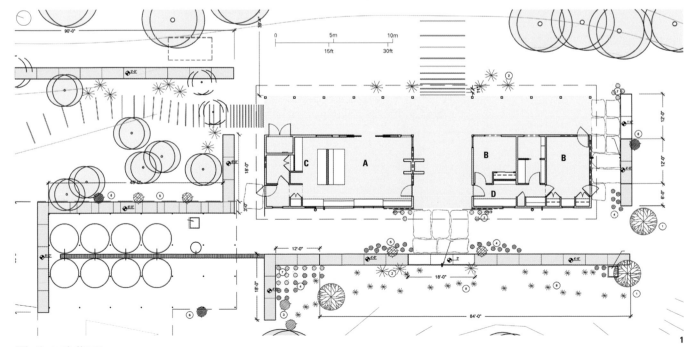

1

1   Floor plan, illustrating the two pavilions set
      beneath a broad mono-pitched roof: [A] living
      room, [B] bedroom, [C] kitchen, [D] studio.
2   Viewed from the side elevation, the extent of
      the roof can clearly be seen.

2

3

4

5

archetypal mono-pitched roof cattle shed. The split between internal and external space is an evolution of the traditional 'dog-trot' typology, which uses a single roof to oversail several enclosed elements surrounded by a covered but open space for livestock.

The other fundamental premise was environmental efficiency. Key elements include a 75,700-litre (20,000-gallon) rainwater collection system, use of recycled materials, soy-based insulation, green 'zero-VOC' (volatile organic compounds) paints, site orientation to encourage natural ventilation, and an air-conditioning system zoned between the two pavilions. The total enclosed

area of the house is around 110 square metres (1200 square feet), covered by 325 square metres (3500 square feet) of roof. The public pavilion contains a kitchen, dining area, utility area ('mudroom') and half-bath, while the private zone contains two bedrooms, a bathroom, a utility room and a home office. There is also an external shower on the covered porch area outside the master bedroom.

Building materials were donated, with local materials used where possible, including recycled wood and stone. The finished product is an environmentally friendly single family house on a relatively remote

rural site, the wooden cladding allowing the house to harmonize with its surroundings. The forms are pared down and elegant, with simple, understated yet carefully considered proportions.

1

HOUSE AND STUDIO

Münsterland, Germany

2000

Léon Wohlage Wernik

Of all the building materials used in contemporary residential architecture, concrete has had the roughest ride. Lambasted for its perceived sterility, coldness and often unhomely feel, it has come to embody the more inhuman aspects of Modern architecture. Yet concrete remains integral to the construction of a vast proportion of housing today, usually shielded and disguised, overclad with a skin of brick or wood, lined and plastered. And, in addition, 'raw' concrete continues to remain dear to a large number of architects, perhaps because it offers unrivalled structural and sculptural possibilities.

This generous 300 square metre (3230 square foot) two-bedroom house and studio in Münsterland, Germany, designed by Berlin-based architects Léon Wohlage Wernik (Hilde Léon, Konrad Wohlage and Siegfried Wernik), was created for a couple who both work from home yet in separate fields. Located in a new suburb, on a plot bordered by a stream and mature trees, the design had to accommodate the closed-off northerly aspect and exploit open views to the south. The plan is arranged on a rigid grid of four units by twelve units, creating a harmonious relationship between the proportions of the key elements:

a living space and two enclosed atriums, one adjacent to the entrance, the other behind the west-facing garden façade. To the south, a patio extends out from the living area.

The structural concrete slabs, laying bare the process of their formation and assembly, dominate every view and are utilized alongside other hard-edged materials to provide a stirring yet sympathetic composition. Steel windows are punched into the walls and are combined with sliding elements that change the composition of the façade, while inside white ceilings, black wenge wood parquet flooring

1   The external courtyard, an austere space
    reached from the main living area.
2-4 Elevations.
5-6 Floor plans: [A] living room, [B] bedroom,
    [C] kitchen, [D] courtyard.

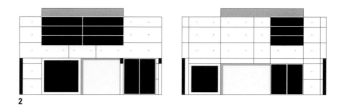

2

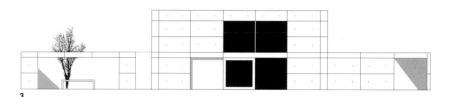

3

4

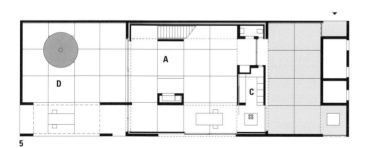

5

0   5m   10m
    15ft   30ft

6

8

9

and ash doors stretch between openings, with no skirtings or extraneous details. The staircase is a strip of folded steel, with the stairwell painted an ethereal blue. External concrete finishes are retained in the bathroom, where the fetishization of raw materials continues – the bath is a large chunk of solid cedar.

Léon Wohlage Wernik speak of 'ambivalence' as a driving force behind the spatial pattern, and the house is full of seemingly contradictory elements. Here is a domestic space hewn from naked slabs of industrial concrete; the space is both office and residence; the views

reach both outside and in thanks to the voids and double-height spaces. There are antecedents to such a creation of external yet internal spaces, linked with the main space through the use of identical materials, and modulating views out to the landscape while allowing in light, most famously Ludwig Mies van der Rohe's Barcelona Pavilion. Léon Wohlage Wernik are similarly concerned with the importance of order and precision, as the floor grid reveals, yet their stated intention is not just to trap and control the views, but to allow for openings and voids that frame vistas from the heart of the house. Fixed

external components such as plinths and tables, all constructed in concrete, serve up monolithic yet scaled-down elements that reflect the house's gridded perfection.

Villa Hoofddorp was the result of a commission for a total work of art, in which every element was designed by the architect. The brief was for a house for a couple with three children (and two dogs), and included a swimming pool, a large garden and the seemingly para-doxical combination of 'an open character with maximum privacy'.

The house is located at Floriande, one of the VINEX sites designated as 'urban expansion areas' by the Dutch government. This site, in Hoofddorp, near to Amsterdam's Schipol Airport, is designated for detached houses. The arrangement of plots is relatively tight, making privacy hard to attain. Verhey has made the rear façade of the cube-shaped building almost completely transparent, with the other sides given a series of slots, arranged to bring light in rather than create views out. Their apparent random arrangement cloaks the house in an air of mystery. Verhey describes this as 'an abstraction that enhances the sculptural effect of the whole'.

External walls are poured shuttered concrete, left unfinished, with the imprints of the bolts that held the shuttering together forming a repeat pattern across the façades. Each of the three storeys is the result of a separate pour, and an

1   A serene vision in exquisitely poured concrete, the Villa Hoofddorp 's street façade is punctuated by a series of carefully composed windows.
2   The garden façade is glazed, yet the windows are contained behind a wall of movable shutters.

VILLA HOOFDDORP

Floriande, Netherlands

2004

Paul Verhey Architecten

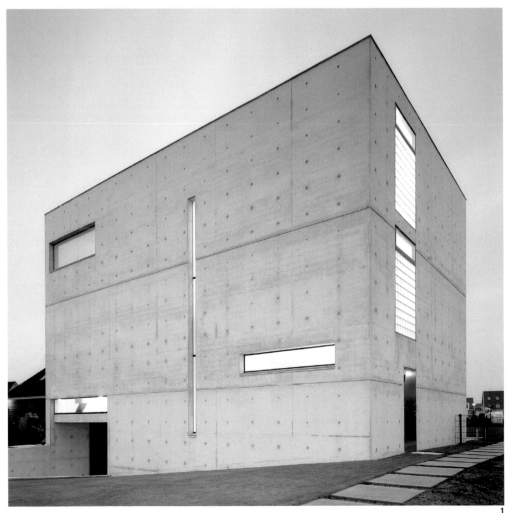

1

3 Floorplans from ground floor up: [A] living
   room, [B] bedroom, [C] kitchen, [D] studio,
   [E] garage, [F] dining room, [G] terrace,
   [H] studio/bedroom.

4 The external staircase running up the east
   façade, past the flush glazing.

5 Inside the main living area, striated by
   sunlight through the wooden shutters.

6 The change of level in the main living area:
   the concrete stairs appear to be carved out of
   the fabric of the house

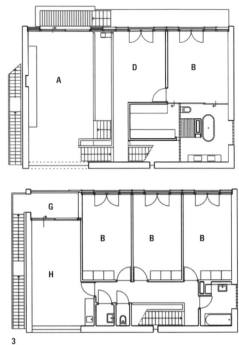

3

0   2.5m   5m
   7.5ft   15ft

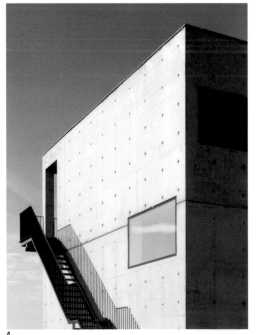

4

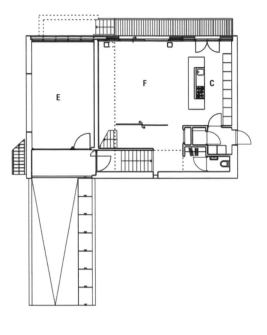

5

6

external seam distinguishes the main level changes within the 400 square metre (1300 square foot) house. There are five internal floor levels, with a double-height living area at the centre. Concrete finishes continue inside, and a cast *in situ* staircase steps down into the living room from the galleried study that is en suite to the master bedroom on level one. On the floor above are three identically sized children's rooms and a study, which can double as a guest bed with private terrace, partly contained within the building's rectangular concrete frame. An external stair runs up the east façade to give the room a separate access.

All residential functions face south, and the glazed façade is covered by a screen of red cedar slats to shield against sun and neighbours. Floor-to-ceiling windows at first- and second-floor level open completely to let in the outside on warm days. The relatively compact footprint has allowed for the maximum garden area, with space for a long lap pool, screened by dense vegetation.

The house is approached from the north, via a sunken entrance and garage. One ascends into an entrance hall and open-plan kitchen and dining area. French doors lead out into the garden, and concrete stairs lead up to the living area, with its own external terrace.

An unconventional suburban home, this is a new interpretation of a housing type that has become the clichéd whipping boy of the architectural establishment. By eschewing conventional materials and external arrangements, the architects have the freedom to devote the house's orientation and internal layout to its site and purpose, creating a private retreat in a crowded world.

BRICK LEAF HOUSE

Hampstead, London, UK

2003

Woolf Architects

This double house occupies the site of a far older structure in Hampstead, North London. Set within the old walled garden, adjacent to surviving outbuildings (adapted to contain parking, an office and a studio), the two new houses can be read as a single volume. The brief called for two separate dwellings, for two brothers and their families. Each is a two-storey house, conventionally organized with four bedrooms above two large living areas. The site steps up steeply from the road, a change in level easily accommodated in the broad sweep of hand-made brick wrapped around the building envelope. The approach rises past the outbuildings, across a surface of granite cobbles, towards the entrance at the 'rear' of the house, with correspondingly fewer windows than on the three garden elevations. The garden wall funnels visitors towards the door, with subtle spatial games concealing the extent of the site and the slight rotation of the nearest house. Its true size is only revealed when viewed from the garden, where the land slips away to the south.

Inside, there are a few shared, interlocking elements subtly integrating the two structures, most importantly the basement pool and gym, a 'cavern-like space' running across beneath each house, illuminated by a glass panel set into the external terrace at first-floor level. This area is accessed via a hidden passage and staircase, described by the architects as a 'family secret'. The pool entrance also provides the step and corridor linkage between the houses, from one entrance hall to another.

For all the size (approximately 930 square metres, 10,000 square feet) and expense, the intention was to avoid costly processes. The houses are built using a structural steel frame, allowing for straightforward alterations. Walls consist of a single leaf of external brickwork, then

1   Floor plans: [A] living room, [B] bedroom,
    [C] kitchen/family room, [D] studio,
    [E] garage/utility, [F] entrance hall, [G] pool,
    [H] nursery.
2   The approach to the twin houses is along a
    cobbled, sloping lane, almost cocooned by
    the brick walls.

insulation and internal blockwork, studded out with plasterboard. Effort was focused on detail rather than craft – the interior is stripped of cornicing and skirtings, with floor-to-ceiling doors and openings maximizing the open feel of the downstairs floor plan. Circulation spaces are at the heart of the plan, lit by a central atrium that continues down to illuminate the pool. Care was taken to differentiate fixtures and layouts; the brothers had no desire to live in mirror-image houses.

The fenestration is simple and unpretentious, and the absence of a parapet results in a stark, modern appearance. 'All domestic brick building in this country is dominated by white framed windows,' Woolf writes, 'and we see no reason to deviate from that.' Luxurious materials were reserved for the 'public' ground-floor spaces – large slabs of *pietra serena* sandstone flooring and dark walnut joinery and flooring. The wooden flooring continues upstairs, with slate in the bathrooms. During the design process, the architects created a beautifully detailed concept model from oak and iroko wood, an emblem of the intentions behind the project. The finished result has a similar hewn quality, a solid mass with an astonishing interior.

3

4

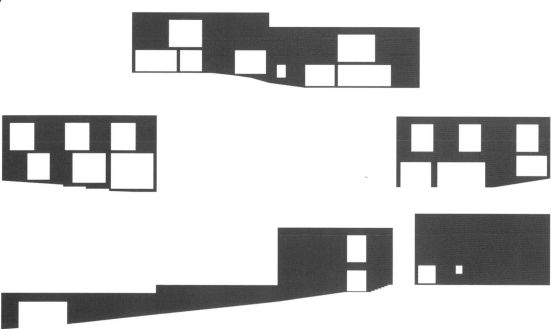

5

1

CAMPEGGIO NEL BOSCO

Collalto Sabino, Italy

2002

**T Studio / Guendalina Salimei
Architetto**

The cabin in the woods has assumed a mythic cultural status, a place to retreat to from contemporary life. Consider the famous building in which Henry David Thoreau composed *Walden* (1854), a humble structure, 'ten feet wide by fifteen long … with a garret and a closet, a large window on each side, one door at the end, and a brick fire opposite'. Thoreau described how he drew pleasure from something so basic, built with natural materials, as part of his withdrawal from a complex and crowded industrial society.

The hut remains a quintessential symbol of a short-term departure from societal norms, whether as a

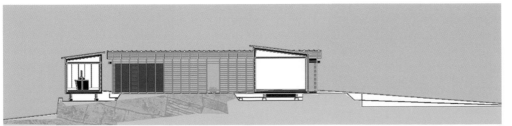

2

3

4

5

seasonal retreat or as an anti-architectural statement, a rejection of the perceived brutality of modern materials and the complexity of current form-making in favour of the honest traditions of wooden construction and enduring simplicity of a pitched roof and four walls.

This project, by the Rome firm T Studio, was for the provision of three service pavilions – a washing block, a toilet block and an open loggia – for a small campsite in Collalto Sabino, a mountain village in central Italy. Local vernacular drives the design, and these wooden buildings derive their form from the rural architecture that pervades this

part of Italy, celebrating irregularity, rough-hewn wood and the juxta-position of vertical structural elements with the surrounding forest. The mono-pitched buildings feature high-level openings for light and ventilation, underlining their seasonal usage.

The campsite itself leads off from the enclosure created by the reception buildings, and is arranged as a group of terraces looping around the curve of a nearby hillock and then cascading down into the valley. The wooden buildings sit lightly on their concrete plinths, raised up to look down the hillside. Admittedly, these are not houses in the

conventional sense – they are not even residential huts. But the combination of scale, materials and site give T Studio's work a domestic feel. The studio is multi-disciplinary, combining landscape, graphic and interior design with architecture; in plan form the campsite reads like a bold graphic element, exaggerating the contours of the site. The all-wood construction lends the struc-tures a certain honesty, and in time the elements will dramatically change the way the fresh, new wood will look.

1 Although located in a small village, the Black House reads best as a solitary, stand-alone object in the landscape.

2 The house is raised up above the ground on a floating foundation like the vernacular storage barns in the region.

3 West elevation: the three floor levels are clearly expressed on the façade.

4 North elevation: the front door.

5 Floor plans: [A] living room, [B] bedroom, [C] kitchen, [D] studio, [E] utility.

1

2

Context is one of the bugbears of new architecture, especially in rural settings. In many countries and communities, planning strictures stipulate that new buildings reflect the architectural vernacular of the local region, in materials, form and scale, removing the opportunity for individual architectural statements. Architectural aesthetics are also politicized, with deviations from what is perceived to be 'normal' frequently pilloried or rejected. Ironically, this recent British project references a recent but largely forgotten past, rather than the timid domestic aesthetic that passes for the contemporary vernacular.

The Black House, located on the flat fens of East Anglia, highlights a problem in domestic architecture; the evaporation of a true vernacular tradition. Built on a new plot on the outskirts of a small Cambridgeshire village near Ely, the Black House is strikingly different from nearby houses, almost all relatively recent, traditionally styled family homes. The newcomer makes its presence felt: rather than utilize harsh new brick, which seems strikingly alien in this featureless landscape, the house is entirely clad in cement fibreboards, waterproofed with a black-hued coating, forming the walls and the roof.

Visually, the Black House has more in common with the barns and agricultural sheds that are prevalent throughout this part of England. The new house is three storeys tall, one more than the standard spec-built homes surrounding it; the additional level is explicitly acknowledged by the line that runs around the building. It is also raised up above the ground, along the lines of the traditional granary. The raised floor serves two practical purposes – it maximizes airflow around the building, helping with ventilation, and avoids the need for a damp-proof course where the house meets the marshy fenland.

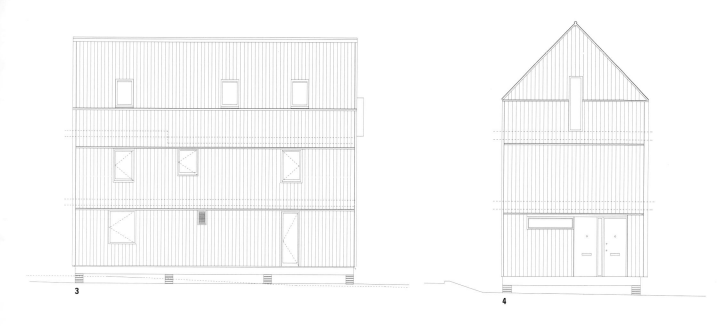

3

4

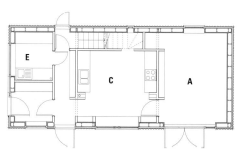

E

C

A

D

B

B

BLACK HOUSE

Cambridgeshire, UK

2002

Meredith Bowles, Mole Architects

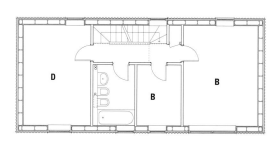

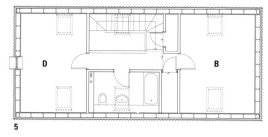

D

B

0   2.5m   5m

7.5ft   15ft

5

6

7

8

Designed by Meredith Bowles of Mole Architects for his young family, the Black House is an object lesson in design modesty and environmental efficiency. The well-insulated walls, the extensive use of recycled timber, and a heat pump all play their part in the efficient use of energy (two thirds of the energy generated in the UK goes into heating houses). The house is west-facing to allow evening sun to heat the interior, and plans are afoot to fit a small, 2-metre (6 foot 6 inch) diameter wind turbine to the roof, which will eventually provide about half of the house's energy. Photovoltaic panels will also be fitted to the south side. The glazing, contained within yellow-stained frames that make bold shapes in the façade, is carefully placed to maximize views across the ploughed fields, and is filled with argon, an inert gas that improves the insulating abilities of the glass.

Bowles built most of the house himself, using hard-wearing materials, put together with care. This self-build, bespoke creation compares well to standard models offered by volume housebuilders; the five-bedroom, 150 square metre (1600 square foot) house, was extremely low-cost, and took around eight months to build. The project won the RIBA's 2004 Manser Medal.

6 The kitchen. Designed and built by the architect for his own family, the house has a consciously domestic feel.

7 The raised foundation provides natural ventilation, aiding the house's impressive environmental performance.

8 The west-facing terrace is accessed by a variety of openings.

9 Eclectic touches, such as this bold patterned wallpaper in the stair lobby, prevent the house becoming a dry modernist statement.

9

the future house

This section considers the role of technology in residential design, along with emerging methods for designing, distributing and manufacturing the twenty-first-century house. The case studies are a mix of built works and concepts, new schemes, technologies, solutions and prototypes, some in the pipeline, some pipe dreams, others frustrated by funding and bureaucracy.

Arguably, all one-off houses are prototypes, but cost usually prohibits avant-garde ideas from filtering down to the mass market. Nonetheless, the twentieth century saw endless speculation on the 'house of the future', placing the home at the core of the consumerist world of tomorrow.[1] 'Future houses' are closely allied to developments in materials and appliance technology, with avant-garde designs used as a means of stimulating future markets and promoting commercial rather than social agendas. But are we better served by a more public radicalism, instead of confining experimentation to the private – and usually wealthy – sphere of the one-off house?

So what is the future of the house? Many have tried to pin down the precise trajectory of tomorrow's residential needs, from those with a vested interest, be they manufacturers, architects or consumers, to doomsayers who predict the imminent decline of conventional social structures. The raw truth of the world's housing market is that convention usually wins out. Despite endless speculation, the family house has not changed much in 100 years, and is unlikely to alter much in the next 100. With such a static market, why is change inevitably discussed in aesthetic terms? This is partly historical, from when Modern designs reacted against social conformity and provoked genuine shock and outrage. As the century progressed, the opposition to new architecture could be attributed

no longer to shock and unfamiliarity but, Modern design's proponents believed, to outdated, anti-progressive thought.

Nothing could be further from the truth. House-builders have a vested interest in technological innovation, improved construction methods and material usage – these all impact on costs. The widely held belief that conventional houses are visually and structurally backward fails to take account of economic forces, although charges of poor environmental performance are more valid. Many architects have long believed that the house-building industry should modernize, bringing on board technology from the motor industry to cater to a rapidly diversifying market. These 'factory-built' homes would be largely prefabricated, fulfilling the old Modernist ideology of the house as a 'machine for living in' [2]. Prefabrication technology, the Holy Grail of the new modernist, is already in widespread use. As Allison Arieff and Bryan Burkhart note in their book on the topic, 'the majority of housing built in the United States and abroad is, to some degree, prefabricated, and the number of prefabricated housing units built is increasing each year'.[2] The modernist prefabricated home is little more than a niche offering. Despite undeniable technological advances (for example Toyota's factory-made homes) the end result remains 'traditional': architects and designers are striving to inject 'design' into a building form that, while Modernist in origins, had managed to shake off any stylistic innovation. This ability to shift shape and accommodate changing taste is also, ironically, a result of the application of manufacturing technology and marketing know-how, for example IKEA's BokLok home, which will be carefully tailored for each marketplace it enters, or the 4 × 8 House with its kit of parts [3].[3]

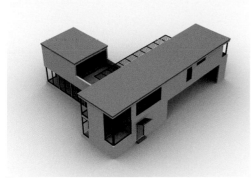

[2] MODERN MODULAR, 2003. Resolution: 4 Architecture

[3] 4 × 8 HOUSE, London, UK, 2004. Project Orange Architects

[4] Q SERIES HOME, Canada, 2004. Kohn Shnier Architects

[5] PREFABRICATED HOUSING, 2003. Rollalong Ltd

[6] QUIK-HOUSE, 2004. Kalkin & Co

Volume house-building is a surprisingly technologically advanced business, yet for the most part, architects and designers feel that the *style* of such housing is sub-standard. This is a cultural, not a technological issue. Arieff and Burkhart argue that modular building can transcend 'workaday' designs, yet while their examples are highly worthy (and photogenic), they rarely address that most thorny of issues: popular taste. There is no real reason why traditional and contemporary designs cannot share space on a housing production line and in a catalogue, in much the same way as sofas do. The implication of such co-existence is that by treating Modernism as just another lifestyle choice, the movement will irrevocably lose its pioneering edge.

For prefabricated projects, economies of scale are crucial. The *Dwell* home uses basic components that can be arranged in a number of ways, and is budgeted at a shade under $200,000 (£105,000); good value, but better value still if a lot of 20 homes were built at the same time. The project's website notes that several volume house-builders have subsequently offered prefab homes in 'modern' designs, including the Q Series from Canada's Royal Homes [4], designed by Kohn Shnier Architects and contrasting strongly with the company's other 'pre-engineered' products with such evocative names as Victorian, Southport, Monarch, Kensington and Citadel.⁴ Technology provides a plurality of aesthetic choice; it does not confirm a hierarchy of style.

Will mass-produced houses ever approach the levels of design integrity, build quality and material efficiency demonstrated by a family saloon car? In their 'Broadside', published in *Blueprint* magazine, James Woudhuysen and Ian Abley put forward a vision of England in 2016: the Thames corridor a hyper-dense conurbation of modular homes, constructed in highly automated factories in almost endless varieties, each type offering its owners a means of customizing, extending and upgrading their dwellings.⁵ Is this a practical view of tomorrow? The 'Broadside' imagined car factories reconfigured to build houses, but devoted little attention to practicalities, consumer desires and the reality of the building industry. Woudhuysen and Abley foresee manufactured homes as the 'giant Apple iPods for their age: powerful, sleek, easy to operate and full of personally selected details. But never modular or plasticky'. The reality is more in line with the Rollalong Pre-fab [5], whereby the chief economic benefits of prefabrication – rapidity and simplicity – are simply applied to the cheapest and least design-intensive housing forms on the market.

'Drag and drop' culture has not had a discernible impact on house-buyers. Modernism's real contemporary legacy is lightweight architecture, which adapts the technological advantages of temporary, often industrial, construction processes for the domestic market. Another popular, if rather theoretical, technology transfer is the shipping container, an admirable consolidation of prefabrication and pragmatism. Countless schemes exist for its adaptation, for instance Sean Godsell's 'FutureShack', exhibited at the Cooper-Hewitt National Design Museum in Washington [1]. However, it is unclear whether there is a true economic benefit in the adaptation of shipping containers or whether this particular fascination is simply the manifestation of a popular cultural meme [6, 7].⁶ The advantages of off-site construction, however, are numerous, and such projects as Rocio Romero's LV Home [8] meld the potentially lower cost of factory manufacturing with the ability to transport the entire structure to site for finishing.

The history of the twentieth-century house was ultimately the history of social attitudes towards technology *within* the home, not a story of advancements in construction or aesthetics. Domestic space was increasingly privatized, with the home as a retreat, a rejection of social engagement. Experience has shown that the market is subject to drastic corrections and reversals, and it is these that pose one of the biggest threats to innovation in housing design. Today's home is a castle to be defended against the unwelcome incursions of the state. In addition, rapid inflation in the value of housing stock over the last 30 years has not been evenly distributed. Modern design has failed – and is still failing – to address these yawning inequalities; it might even be exacerbating the problem.

Add to this swiftly changing demographics, in particular the fragmentation of the extended family unit in favour of the single family household. In Britain, house sizes are shrinking as a result: the average three-bedroom dwelling dropped from around 100 square metres (1000 square feet) in the 1930s to 80 square metres (860 square feet) in the 1980s. Today, it is around about 60 square metres (650 square feet), testament to the economic pressures facing house-builders. Conversely, in America, where economic and space pressures are not as great, houses are expanding in size.[7]

Technology, far from blending seamlessly into the background, is being pushed to the fore, yet we are still a long way from the fulfilment of the 'digital glamour' era, when the gap between the seductive yet unbuildable rendered image is finally equalled – and perhaps surpassed – by new works that use computers at all stages of the process to create genuinely new environments.[8] The 'new pragmatic' architecture set out in the previous chapter contrasts strongly with the emerging market for 'techno-houses', information-drenched residences that foresee a tomorrow of embedded processors, smart fabrics, display panels and total integration with digital culture [9]. In addition, the so-called 'smart house', like the ongoing MIT House_N testbed project, does not discriminate on stylistic grounds. The technology that inhabits our daily lives is not even especially bothered by the technology of construction, and the 'home theatre' or wireless network is just as likely to be part of a shiny new McMansion as a low-cost stylistic experiment, perhaps even more so.

Similarly, advances in construction technology serve to facilitate all types of architecture. Even the ersatz 'period' house, for all its authentic features, is awash with contemporary technology: it is misleading to suggest that today's 'traditional' architecture has anything more than a passing connection to the past, and a tenuous visual one at that. Granted, some ancient construction methods and materials remain in use or are occasionally revived. Timber frame construction or monumental brick construction can result in low-cost and high-performance structures – the abandonment of these methods for an arbitrary notion of 'progress' would be insane. Wisely, many of the more imaginary contemporary solutions, especially in the more pragmatic field, explore traditional construction [10].

While domestic technology serves only to offer increased opportunities for consumption, it is the obsession with skin and surface that remains at the forefront of avant-garde discussions about the single family house. However, the skins in question are stretched and skewed in virtual space, and there remains a largely unbridged gap between theory and practice. Admittedly, one of the key benefits of

[7] CONTAINER CITY, London, UK, 2002. Urban Space Management

[8] LV HOME, 2002. Rocio Romero Design

[9] STYLE HOUSE – PURE/FUN/POP, 2001. Hackenbroich Architekten

the modern media's fascination with architecture and design is that contemporary debate about domestic architecture has been imbued with both a deep respect for the past and a willingness to be experimental and idiosyncratic.

Given the technologically determinist view of the future that dominates contemporary culture, evidence suggests that enthusiasm for adhocism, low-tech and individuality will be driven not by the ongoing failure of 'modern' design to engage the mass market, but by other global factors that will rein in consumption patterns and encourage localized communities. The house of the future will continue to look much like the house of today, with a small proportion of aspirational objects drawn from the avant-garde at the top end of the market. Slowly and surely, society's changing perceptions, projections and predictions for the house of tomorrow will evolve and impact on day-to-day requirements. By 2101, when the first true histories of the twenty-first-century house come to be written, the disparity between the reality on the ground and the shiny visions dreamt up by architectural futurists promises to be all too apparent.

1   See for example Beatriz Colomina, Annmarie Brennan and Jeannie Kim, eds., *Cold War Hothouses*, Princeton Architectural Press, Princeton NJ, 2004, p.103.

2   See Allison Arieff and Bryan Burkhart, *Pre-Fab*, Gibbs Smith Publishers, Salt Lake City, 2002.

3   www.boklok.com.

4   www.royalhomes.com/models/royalqseries/entrance.

5   James Woudhuysen and Ian Abley, *Homes 2016*, Blueprint Broadside, pamphlet accompanying *Blueprint* magazine, September 2004.

6   Container City, in East London (www.containercity.com) contains not homes, but design studios. The Office of Mobile Design (www.designmobile.com) proposes a similar community with their 'Eco-Ville' project, 40 portable units for artists-in-residence on a downtown Los Angeles site. Other container-based proposals have been suggested by the Dutch firm MVRDV (www.mvrdv.nl) and by Shigeru Ban, whose container-based installation occupied Pier 54 in Chelsea, New York, from March to June 2005.

7   'The National Association of Home Builders' "showcase home" for 2005 is 5,950 sq. ft. [550 sq. m.]. That's 15% bigger than last year's model.' 'This New House', *Mother Jones*, March/April 2005

8   Joseph Rosa, ed., *Glamour: Fashion and Industrial Design and Architecture*, Yale University Press, New Haven CT and London, 2004, p.131.

[10] GLIDEHOUSE, California and Washington, USA, 2004. Michelle Kaufmann Designs

PALM SPRINGS MODULAR HOUSE

Slovenia

2001

Maechtig Vrhunc Arhitekti

The Palm Springs Modular House was the joint first-prize-winner in a 2001 open competition. Organized by the Slovenian timber company RIKO, which builds its prefabricated 'Eco-House' for the German and Austrian domestic market, the competition sought new approaches to the age-old issue of prefabrication in housing design, a technology that has failed to keep abreast of contemporary aesthetic developments.

Designed by Slovenian architects Maechtig Vrhunc Arhitekti (MVA), the Modular House uses the principle of standardized, scalable components, allowing common parts to form four differently sized

houses, A2, A3, A4 and A6, ranging from 53.3 to 129.4 square metres (575 to 1390 square feet). Each modular home is structured around a base element, a simple ground-floor plan that can be added to or subtracted from as desired. MVA's design uses prefabricated wooden panels for the floors, walls, structure and roof. Façades are then clad with a thick layer of copper. All construction was intended to be undertaken in the factory, with CAD files translated into computer-aided manufacturing and produced on a three-axis milling machine.

The dream of the mass-produced home has long occupied architects

and designers. In the past century, the utopian vision was of the house as machine, a structure that would be the ultimate affirmation of Le Corbusier's (in)famous pronouncement, combined with the freshly evolved technology of the construction line, enabling houses to be churned out like motor cars and finished to similar standards. Countless architects busied themselves with designs that would cross over between the two worlds, including Buckminster Fuller and his circular metal Dymaxion House of 1946, and the Finnish architect Matti Suuronen with his plastic-shelled Futuro House of 1968.

1

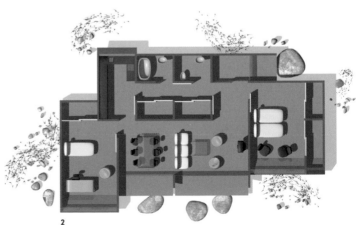

2

Today's prefabrication systems are sophisticated and cost-efficient, but the systems devised by such companies as PortaKabin eschew radical floor plans and materials in favour of conservatively styled modular components. Even this is not sober enough for the majority of the world's housing markets, however, and prefabrication is generally confined to office construction or the creation of dedicated components such as bathrooms and kitchens. Attempts to integrate prefabrication into housing production are progressing slowly, despite the recommendations of a number of reports advocating higher take-up of techniques evolved in the motor industry.

MVA's design uses wood, perhaps the most suitable material for the prefabrication of housing (and, ironically, totally unrelated to the technologies usually associated with automobiles). In countries with a strong tradition of wooden architecture, prefabrication technologies are sophisticated, matching the warmth of a traditional material with its flexibility, transportability and affordability. The work of Austrian architect Oskar Leo Kaufmann, for example, exemplifies the way in which factory-finished wooden panels can be integrated into sophisticated architectural compositions. Maechtig Vrhunc Arhitekti's Palm Springs design continues this tradition, creating a truly modern architecture that has widespread applications for mass-produced housing.

1 Roofscape.
2 Rendered floor plan: the house is reduced to product, with various plug-in add-ons to expand the space.
3 Viewed from outside in this series of computer renders, the Palm Springs Modular House has angular, futuristic aspects.

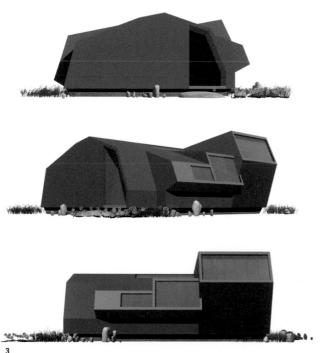

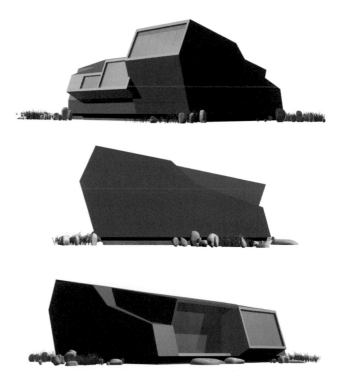

3

1

M7 PROTOTYPE

Tunquén, Chile

2004

URO1.ORG

The M7 Prototype house project encap-sulates the key issues surrounding the call for greater prefabrication in domestic architecture, namely practicality and cost. Ostensibly a project for a holiday home in Chile's wild Tunquén region, overlooking the Pacific coast, the house was designed by the URO1.ORG cooperative of architects and designers.

The structure was designed to consist of 27 prefabricated units, all of which would be manufactured in Santiago and then transported to the site and assembled, using just screws and drills and no wet processes. This modular system

provided an almost infinite variety of building solutions from just a few standardized components. Construction took a mere nine days. Each module comprised two 21-millimetre (13/16 inch) glued plywood planks, carefully prepared by a cabinet-maker to form a repeatable element, 240 × 40 centimetres (95 × 16 inches), that forms both structure and skin, interlocking to provide a variety of internal and external spaces. The advantages of this structure/skin combination are that interior and exterior are fused, and the house is complete as soon as construction is finished. Internal furnishings become part of the main

build, and such elements as shelves and storage are integrated.

The asymmetry of the construction unit encouraged experimentation, and there is a variety of floor levels and vertical surfaces within the house. Windows frame views across the barren landscape, while frames form shelving and storage. The low cost and the fact that the architects also acted as the workforce resulted in innumerable delays: at one stage, the partially completed house stood open to the elements for an entire winter, yet although the plywood was beaten and worn, its structural integrity remained. The finished product

2

1-2 Made up of 27 pre-fabricated elements, the
M7 Prototype has weathered swiftly in its
position on the Pacific coast.

3 The newly finished house had a very different
character from the current structure.

4 The prefabricated sections form both internal
and external elements, including shelving
and window slots.

3

4

is clad in a resin formed from fibre-glass, further weatherproofing the house.

At 45 square metres (485 square feet), and with a total budget of less than $10,000 (approximately 7,800 euros or £5,400), the M7 is a far cry from the conventional Modernist beach house (of which numerous examples litter the surrounding countryside), recalling instead the ad hoc shacks found in traditional fishing colonies. Its prototypical nature is displayed both in the rough-and-ready finishes and exterior and in the unfolding, undisciplined nature of the internal spaces. As a result, the M7 Prototype has an experi-mental, avant-garde aspect, recalling the sculptural experiments in form and space that were undertaken by the Russian Constructivists, which had a major impact on International Modernism's approach to domestic space. The architect Gerrit Rietveld is another significant point of reference, in particular his Schroeder House of 1923–4, which dispensed with the usual hierarchy of rooms and service spaces in favour of transformable open-plan living.

The URO1.ORG cooperative has gone on to develop a production-ready prefabrication system, known as MN PRO, which builds on the techniques and problems that were uncovered during the M7 project, to make a practical, low-cost building product. Of the 167 boards used to form the 27 units of the M7 Prototype, only half a board went to waste, making this an exercise in pure, yet highly efficient, space.

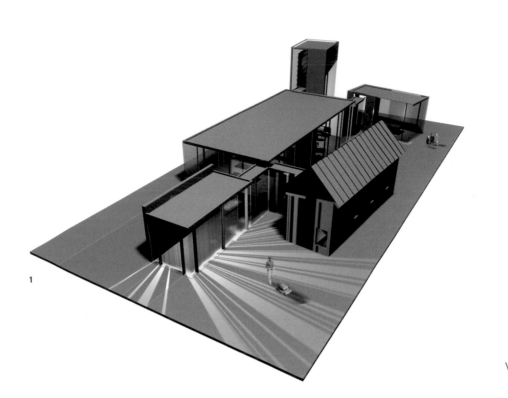

**TWENTY
PROPOSITIONS
FOR SUBURBAN
LIVING**

Raleigh, North Carolina, USA

2001

Borden Partnership LLP

1

The American suburb is a familiar
space, the apogee of the American
dream, and the picket fence and
clapboard screen that shields its
nightmares. In the half-century since
modern architecture evolved into its
current form, the archetypal house
has barely changed. There may be
countless types of suburban house,
but the overwhelming aesthetic
preference is for traditional styles,
tweaked for the modern age. This
infuriates many architects. That
suburbia should have evolved into
the best combination of location and
aspiration without expressing a
more overt desire for modern living
is a source of ongoing confusion.

Gail Peter Borden's 'Twenty
Propositions for Suburban Living'
takes as its starting point the origins
of American suburbanism, engaging
with what exists without disparaging
the benefits of the experience.
Borden's team estimated the median
value of the average American home
– a three-bedroom home on an 18 ×
37 metre (60 × 120 foot) lot –
providing parameters within which
to work. Yet, rather than consider the
house as an artefact to be 'evolved',
he re-examined a series of crucial
conditions, including typology,
material, cost, public/private space,
different uses during day and night,
services and serviced areas.

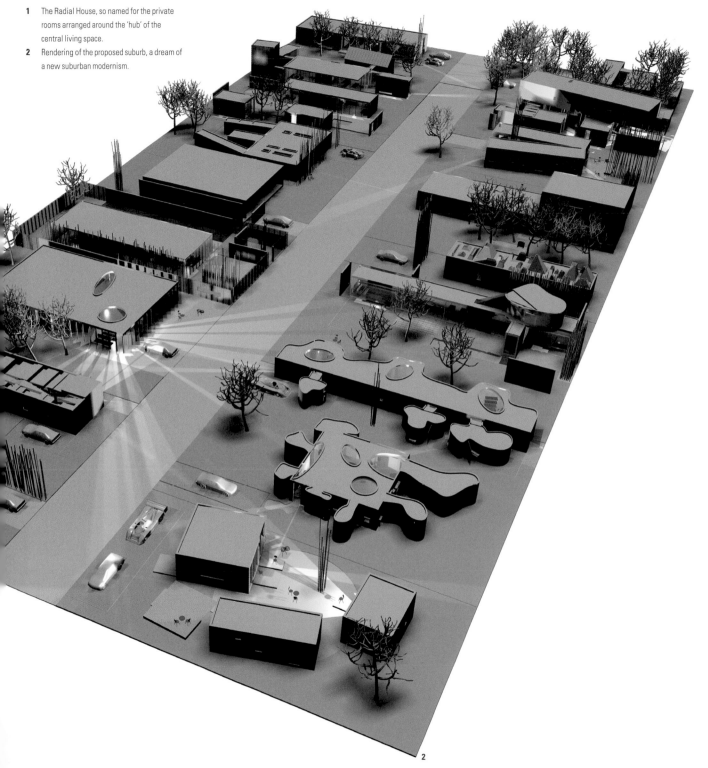

1 The Radial House, so named for the private rooms arranged around the 'hub' of the central living space.

2 Rendering of the proposed suburb, a dream of a new suburban modernism.

2

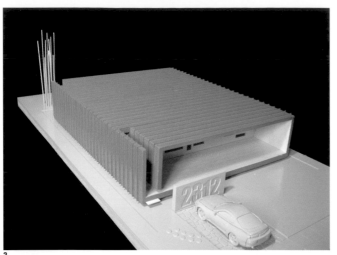

3

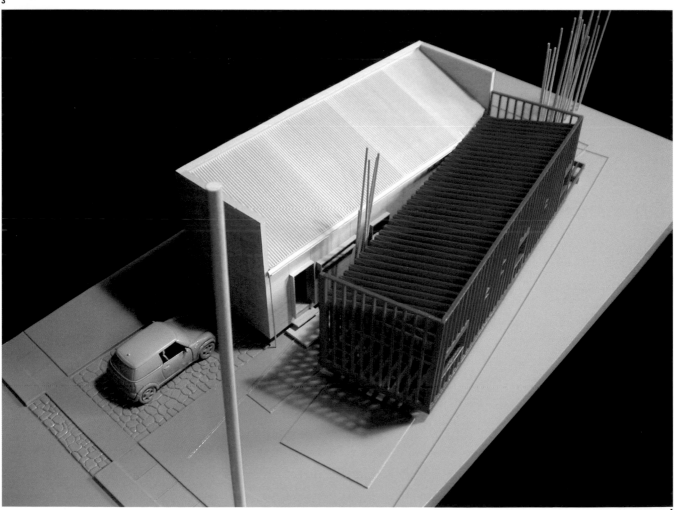

4

3 The ultra-private Enclosure House, with its wrap-around 'skin' that seamlessly envelops the entire living area.

4 The Gradient House: twin structures, one public, one private, set at a slight angle to one another. The open-plan living room is at left.

5 The Constellation House: a dwelling that draws its inspiration from installation art, with a dynamic roofscape creating a remarkable quality of internal light.

The results are 20 prototype houses that use conventional materials in an 'unconventional way', their layouts zoned, with services tightly grouped to maximize floor area and ensure a better interplay between internal and external spaces. They are designed to be modular, adapting with changing circumstances, encouraging long-term ownership and greater investment in community.

As its name suggests, the size and uses of the Program House can be articulated over time, as its individual pavilions, beneath an oversailing residential component, are without defined functions. The Gradient House divides public and private into two off-set pavilions, open-plan and compartmentalized respectively. The Porch House builds on the traditional veranda, connecting house and landscape through the large open-air deck running through the property. Again, living spaces are subdivided in pavilions for eating, living and sleeping.

Functional requirements are at the heart of the Tube House, one of the more overtly contemporary designs, with its corrugated metal-clad exterior. In direct contravention of conventional arrangements for open-plan living, the Tube House compartmentalizes living functions along its narrow footprint, in what Borden describes as 'a cul-de-sac of daily activity'. The Constellation House features a dynamic roofscape of rooflights and shapes, making the quality of the interior elusive and shifting, while the internal spaces of the Enclosure House are enveloped in a metal skin, articulated by punched windows at the front and rear and serviced by an internal core.

Borden's aesthetic is modern, with sufficient variety to cater for the contemporary consumer's expectancy of choice. But there are wider debates at play. Do most people want houses that represent rapid cultural change? Is the house the ultimate symbol of cultural memory, a constant that does not change while all around it is in flux? 'Twenty Propositions' does not promise to solve problems, but to provide an alternative that redefines the architectural 'everyday' and enhances communities.

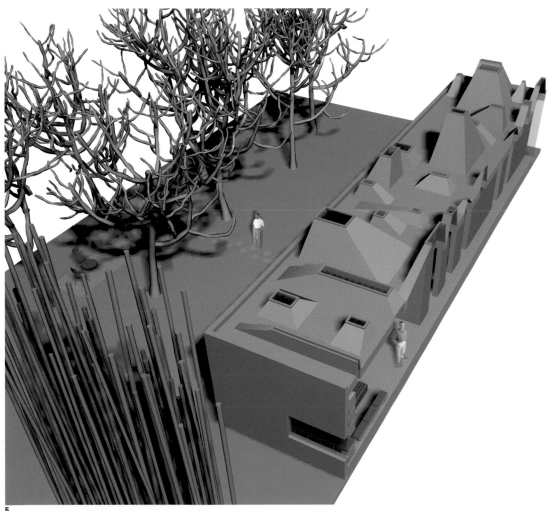

With Parasite Paradise, 23 practi-tioners from the fringes of current architectural and artistic practice sifted through the remnants of one of the last century's most enduring architectural myths, the instant environment. Late Modernism exhibited a fascination with the portable dwelling: devices that could be prefabricated, dropped in – preferably by helicopter – used, then zipped up and taken away.

The Dutch government began sponsoring VINEX zones of urban development in the early 1990s, aiming to create 635,000 new homes by 2005, focusing on 16 'growth centre' municipalities.

At its heart this was a socially progressive programme to deliver new housing, fusing traditional street patterns with high-quality modern design to maintain high densities and minimize car use. Leidsche Rijn was one such centre, filled with 30,000 largely Modernist housing units.

The Parasite Paradise project ('Prototypes for Amphibious Readymade Advanced Smallscale Individual Temporary Ecological Houses') melded Modernist optimism with fine art practice and the reality of nomadic, temporary housing structures, and had its origins in an exhibition at the Stork

grounds, three vast artificial islands of industrial buildings near Amsterdam. In these sheds, an exhibition of relocatable structures was mounted, to be experienced by visitors at 1:1 scale. This led to the Leidsche Rijn experiment, a cultural event that addressed head-on the complex relationship between planned public and private space, a pre-eminent preoccupation of recent architectural practice in the cramped, highly zoned Netherlands.

The fundamental issues raised by the Parasite installations centre on the nature of space, ownership, and freedom to build what one likes where one likes, taking the anarchic

origins of free communities and highlighting disparities between landowners and the dispossessed. The paradox of the 'free state' being determined and contained within a planned zone was not overlooked.

Not all the projects put forward were residential, some countering the criticism of residents about the clustered services offered by the new developments. In a fast-developing world, where hinterland spaces – gaps between motorways, railway lines, industrial estates and box stores – are marginalized, deemed unusable and unwanted, a grass-roots approach that addresses the idea of parasitic, demountable

1

architecture to fill these voids offers benefits for all.

Parasites differ markedly from the Modernist vision of the prefabricated building. Gone is the machine-like rigour of Matti Suuronen's 1968 Futuro House. Instead, structures draw inspiration from caravans and shacks, tents and tepees, as well as the shipping container and even the PortaKabin. The exhibition brought together a number of designs from the last quarter of the twentieth century, from the development of existing technology to provocative yet practical structures that gently question the utility of existing social structures.

Atelier van Lieshout's 2000 'Pioniersset' brought together a lorry's worth of functional components, arranged to create a traditional smallholding, including chicken run, pigsties and rabbit hutches. This romantic view of a preindustrialized industry suggests that a rural utopia is achievable. Eduard Böhtlingk's 'Markies', like several of the projects, uses simple technology to transform its immediate environment, with two concertina-like awnings descending from either side of the basic cabin structure, trebling the floor area.

Other works were starker, using the bare minimum of materials and 'design'. Several used existing elements to form new structures, notably Luc Deleu's 'Orbino', a tower made from five standard-sized international shipping containers, critiquing the standardization and anonymity of global trade.

Ironically, the Leidsche Rijn area saw rumblings of unrest over planning contraventions, as residents sought to erect their own fences without conforming to the original design codes. Even individualism invites regulation.

1 Markies, a fold-out holiday house designed by Eduard Böhtlingk and first exhibited in 1985.

2 Essentially a compact, caravan-like structure, the accordion-like side panels fold down to create nearly 30 square metres (320 square feet) of floor area.

3 One element of Atelier van Lieshout's 2000 project, Pioniersset, a 'mobile farm' comprising stable, sties, hutches and fencing.

PARASITE PARADISE

Leidsche Rijn, Utrecht, Netherlands

2000–

Various architects and artists

2

3

1

UP!HOUSE

USA

2003

Craig Konyk Architecture

Commissioned by *Dwell* magazine as part of an invited competition investigating the contemporary prefab, Craig Konyk Architecture designed the up!house in 2003. They describe it as 'an attempt to make the purchase of the single family house more akin to that of the latest model [Volkswagen] Jetta'. Structurally, the concept is advanced. The house is effectively a see-saw, with a central structural component acting as an anchor with two equally weighted wings counterbalancing each other on either side. This system, developed with Cristobal Correa from engineers Buro Happold, was adopted so as to

minimize on-site preparatory work, with the bonus of the cantilevers providing car ports. The entire house would only require two concrete walls to support its mass.

The interstitial space created by this arrangement not only contains services, concealed behind illuminated cladding, but provides natural ventilation and additional storage. The upper section, a lightweight steel box beam structure, is described as a 'chassis'. The design is modular, with four different sizes offered (the two-bedroom, 140 square metre [1500 square foot] up!3, through to up!9). Plug-in UP and UNDER extensions to the main

beam provide a penthouse or an underslung home theatre. The metal structure is infilled with a highdensity polystyrene-bonded sandwich panel, plastic-coated with UV-resistant automotive-quality sealant.

This kind of factory construction is not new; many conventional homes contain a large proportion of prefabricated components, and apartment buildings are increasingly stitched together from modular elements manufactured off-site, including whole kitchens, bathrooms and living areas. Where the up!house departs from recent usage is in its wholesale adoption of automotive conventions. This is

1. Designed to be built off-site, then transported in pieces to the site, the up!house concept is flexible rather than site-specific.
2. Rendered section through a typical unit: the second bedroom is contained within a raised 'mezzanine', and the sandwich panel construction can clearly be seen.
3. The proposal's 'openable moonroof', which exploits the rigidity of the structural frame.
4. An open-tread stair in the open-plan living area leads up to the mezzanine.

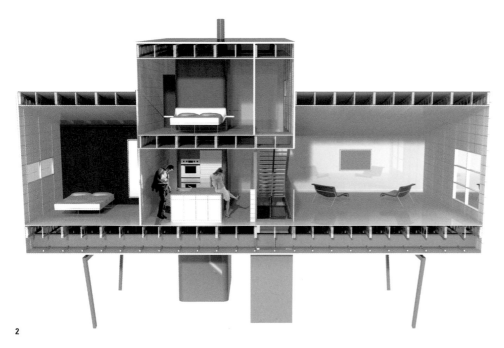

2

a product specified as if from a car showroom, with decisions made online (www.up-house.com) and menus and check boxes offering options 'to suit every pocket'. The finished product would be delivered on the back of a truck for ultra-quick installation on pre-prepared foundations. The ultimate goal would be to create a product that people could take with them when they moved. Initial costings for the up!house proved expensive, demonstrating that regardless of interest generated, manufacturing methods, costings and quantities are integral to the project's success.

Several of the prototypical projects illustrated in this book are modern interpretations of the off-the-shelf home. This is not a new concept; certain twentieth-century architects spent large parts of their careers trying to advance Le Corbusier's dictum that 'a house is a machine for living in', searching for a way to mechanize the process of construction. Few managed to combine such practicalities with the machined aesthetic generally favoured by the Modern Movement; even fewer succeeded in creating a lasting legacy of mass-produced homes. The twenty-first century offers not only more advanced

production machinery, but also the crucial means of disseminating and delivering such ideas: the internet. It remains to be seen whether the house as consumer product is a viable area of development.

3

4

1 West façade: House D sits on a sloping site, a series of five 'ribbons' that gradually uncurl as they step down the hillside to reveal a terrace and pool.

2-3 North and south façades: the upper levels have aesthetic parallels with traditional pitched-roof rural architecture.

4 The pool is contained within a giant steel and concrete shell that cantilevers out over the site and garage below.

5 Floor plan of living/swiming level: [A] living room, [B] swimming pool, [C] kitchen, [D] terrace, [E] storage/utility.

HOUSE D

Velenje, Slovenia

2003

Sadar Vuga Arhitekti

Slovenian studio Sadar Vuga Arhitekti was founded in 1996 by Jurij Sadar and Boštjan Vuga. Together with Miha Pešec and Adrian Petrucelli, they have earned a reputation as demanding, innovative architects, unafraid to question conventional use of form and materials.

House D is their first major residential project. A family home, it addresses its steep site with a cascading form of clearly defined elements. Embedded in the slope is a concrete plinth, above which sits a thick concrete platform. Above that a series of 'strips' wraps around the living spaces, doubling as structural enclosures. This results in four distinct façades. To the north is a relatively conventional 'local' elevation with two storeys addressing nearby buildings, and the first floor set back beneath a broad, shallow-pitched roof. This echoes rural Slovenian architecture, although the steeply raked support column and the floor-to-ceiling glazing hint at subversion.

Each façade is separate, with little clue as to the architectural composition around the corner. The 'strip' system opens up the west façade, and can be read on design sketches and models as a series of petals bursting open to deliver a view. To the east is the 'abstract' façade, a closed series of vertical panels – the start of the strips – arranged in a monolithic progression striding up the hill. To the south is the 'Californian' façade, where the bulk of the house rises up above the sunken garage, and the cascading floor plans culminate in a swimming pool and pavilion, cantilevered out to the west on vast steel brackets, engineered by Jani Ramsak.

The entrance is sheltered beneath the swimming pool cantilever, with a separate path running up the hillside to the 'traditional' façade at the top. Each of the five storeys in the 250 square metre (2690 square feet) house is a separate functional zone.

1

2

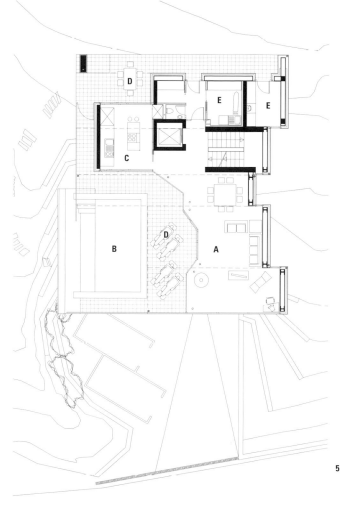

Starting with the garage and storeroom on the ground floor, one ascends to a games room, then to a floor devoted to the children, then to the main living area. Here the kitchen and seating areas step down to a pool, all surrounded by a terrace snaking around the perimeter. The top storey, tucked beneath the roof on the 'traditional' side of the house, contains the master suite, with views across the valley. The roofscape is formed by the petal strips, which flex and twist at varying angles, allowing slots of clerestory glazing to illuminate the living area. The strips are clad in black-coloured bitumen tiles, which combine with a structural steel frame and brick and concrete walls, all sitting on the main slab above the garage.

The architects describe the location as 'very generic Slovenian semi-rural suburbia', and in this context the house offers a visual futurism based on the gradual unwinding of plans and elevations, not wedded to any one form of domestic symbolism. The design is unafraid of bursting – quite literally – out of the Modernist box, while simultaneously complementing and challenging its surroundings.

1. The Eldorado Canyon Residence addresses the topography of its remarkable site with a series of cascading levels and walkways.

2-3. Despite its dramatic presence, the house sits lightly on this remote and spectacular site; the raised walkway minimizes contact with the ground.

4. Floor plans: [A] living room, [B] bedroom, [C] kitchen, [D] studio, [E] garage/utility, [F] art gallery, [G] terrace, [I] swimming pool.

1

2

3

The twenty-first-century house undoubtedly benefits from the gradual democratization of design culture. However, the ultra-high end Modernist villa continues to haunt the popular imagination, an élitist space that is propagated as aspirational. Such houses are the spiritual heirs to the mansion, the country house and even the ancestral seat – super-residences that decry the populist stylings of the McMansion in favour of a more abstract approach, directly evolved from flat-roofed, stripped-down Modernism, with a dose of structural innovation thrown in. There will always be a market for the modern house as spectacular, an architectural special effect that uses Modernist visual and technical language yet is ultimately about display and drama.

At first glimpse, Building Studio's proposed Eldorado Canyon Residence in Colorado ticks all these boxes. The site has an awesome natural beauty, and the brief called for a design of great sculptural intensity, with extensive living spaces (including a separate office, a conference area, an art gallery, a pool and a gymnasium). Yet the house is designed to touch its site lightly and be as environmentally self-sufficient as possible.

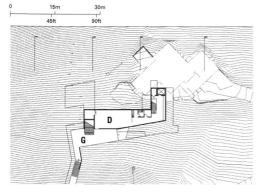

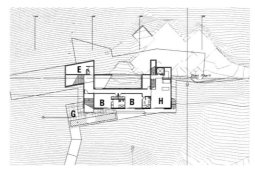

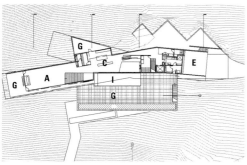

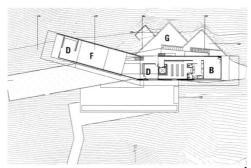

ELDORADO CANYON RESIDENCE

Boulder County, Colorado, USA

2005–

Building Studio

4

The location is remote, on the edge of the Rocky Mountain Front Range, near just a handful of other houses, none of which is visible from the site. Surrounded by the Eldorado Canyon State Park and reached only by a road running through a gravel gorge, the 8-hectare (20-acre) site is steep and awkward. The architects' response is to create a stepped structure, four large concrete 'bars' that minimize ground contact – each supports a major element of the house, arranged as four linear components that follow the contours of the site.

Each component has a concrete floor, a north wall and an oversailing roof slab, creating shade for the extensively glazed south façade. Additional sun-shading is created by the rolling screens constructed from Cor-ten steel, referencing traditional Japanese *shoji* screens. A dramatic 'skywalk' reaches down the hill to the south, a covered structure 30 metres (100 feet) long. Each floor slab has its own terrace at the east–west end, covered for protection from the elements.

The office and conference space is separate from the rest of the dwelling, and is located on the lowest slab. As one climbs higher, the main living spaces unfold; first, guest accommodation and gym, then, on the level above, which also contains garaging, are the kitchen, dining and living area, and swimming pool. The master suite, along with the gallery, is on the upper level along with the inevitable hot tub.

Each level is given what the architects describe as an 'eco-environment'. A deck area with indigenous planting is located off the guest bedroom slab, while there is also a kitchen garden, and a miniature meadow of prairie grass outside the gallery level. At the very top of the house, a Zen-type rock garden will be created.

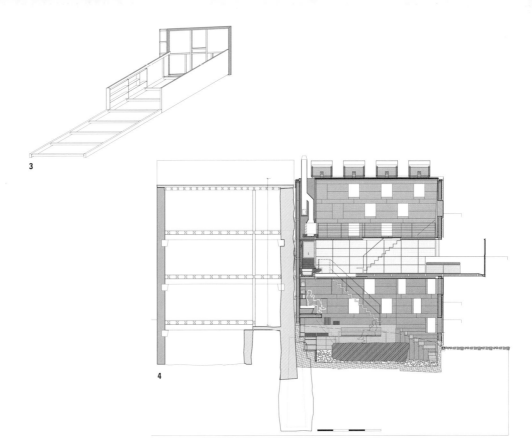

3

4

LIVING ROOM HOUSE

Gelnhausen, Germany

2004

Seifert and Stöckmann Architekten

2

The Living Room is not a house in the conventional sense. Conceived as an artwork/installation, it was a collaboration between architects Gabriela Seifert and Götz Stöckmann and a collective of artists and a poet. Located in Gelnhausen, a medieval town east of Frankfurt, it is awash in visual and poetic metaphors, a structure with dual, even triple meanings – from the outset the architects set out to create an artwork that was integral to, but not dependent on, the form of the domestic house.

The façade is punched through with an array of square windows, with deep sills doubling as shelving

and display spaces. They provide fractured views both inside and out, adding to the house's mystery for pedestrians, who are drawn into the architecture, wondering whether this is a house, an office, or a gallery. In truth, it is all three.

The most dramatic element is the 'living-room shelf', a 2.75-metre (9-foot) balcony that extends electrically from the second storey of the front façade, jutting out above the street. This gesture is practical and playful, transforming the master bedroom into an outside space, while also providing animation and amusement for pedestrians. Local planners were surprisingly sympathetic to such an

avant-garde proposal, and the house now features on the local tourist map, accepted as both as domestic space and an art object.

The living area is in the eaves of the house, where the punched window treatment continues, giving the tight apex of the roof an airy feeling; access is via a trapdoor in the floor. Two daybeds are pushed against a wall of internal wooden shingles, their subtle modulations mirroring the jumble of medieval roofs outside.

The ground floor is given over to a 'landscape', complete with an undulating boulder that forms a natural floor, surrounded by gravel

5

6

paths. The playful nature of the gesture is obvious – 'passers-by can look inside and see what they would expect to find outside,' say the architects. This slab is no superficial piece of rock; it weighs 40 tonnes and was ceremoniously craned into the site at the start of the project. A gallery level overlooks the double-height 'stone level', with extensive concealed storage and shelving. All the function is relegated to this side of the plan. The private spaces are contained within a box suspended directly above the 'landscape', which is reached by a simple straight-run steel staircase.

Stöckmann and Seifert founded Formalhaut in 1985 with Ottmar Horl, and the Living Room House was designed for their own use. The spaces are occasionally allowed to transcend domestic conventions. Nonetheless, this is a complex jigsaw of interlocking space, making the most of a relatively tight, steep corner site.

A series of artworks inspired by the house, including light installations by Frankfurt artist Charly Steiger, adorns the structure. The Living Room House offers a contemporary interpretation of the Arts and Crafts Movement's maxim that a house could be a total work of art – a *Gesamkunstwerk*. Systems building, tough planning conditions, tight budgets and a paucity of skilled trade have made this concept not only unfashionable but also increasingly unattainable in the modern age.

7

5-6 The galleried living space in the eaves of the house, showing the shingle-clad wall and the trap-door access.

7 The deep sills of the grid of windows act as display and storage spaces.

8 The kitchen at ground-floor level, with the floor replaced by a 'boulder landscape'.

9 The 'drawer level' from within, drawer closed. A simple folded steel staircase leads up to the living area in the apex of the roof.

10 The 'drawer level' from within, drawer open.

8

9

10

FISHERMAN'S HOUSE

Asti, Piedmont, Italy

2002

Elastico with Cesario Carena

The phrase 'concrete truffle' is not especially ripe with architectural potential. Yet the firm of Elastico Spazio insists that this is exactly what it has created. For the Fisherman's House is not a conventional structure, even by the standards of the contemporary avant-garde.

Simone Carena and Stefano Pujatti of Elastico have enhanced an existing guardhouse for an extensive private park near the Italian town of Asti in Piedmont. This building is situated close to a main villa and two 1970s houses designed by architect Cesario Carena. Carena was approached to restore the guard-

house and subsequently collaborated with Turin-based Elastico Spazio to create a new addition.

The extension is largely constructed from concrete, a tribute to Carena's earlier villas and a chance to use the material with a sculptural, tectonic form that seems to grow from the landscape. The extension redefines the spatial role of the original structure, opening it up to the park and reading as a series of pavilions stepping down a newly created landscaped slope. The principal feature is a 7-metre (23-foot) cantilever at first-floor level, jutting out over the south-facing lawns. Here there is a new entrance,

1   An eclectic selection of pavilions and additions, the Fisherman's House represents an ongoing refurbishment and new-build project.

2   Floor plans: [A] living room, [B] bedroom, [C] kitchen/dining, [D] courtyard, [E] garage, [F] terrace.

1

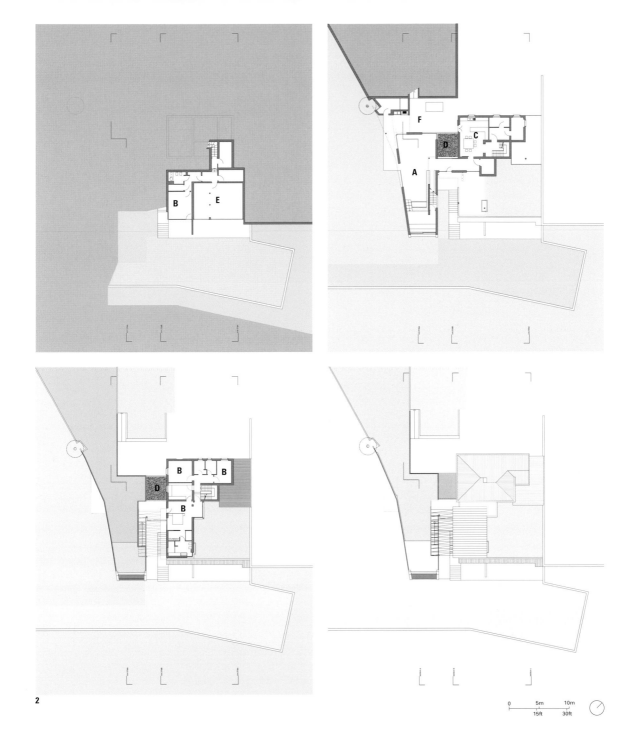

3 Section through the house, showing the original structure and the additions overlooking the garden.

4 The internal courtyard between the old and the new house.

5 The new living room juts out over the garden. It has a green roof and houses a gym and garage below.

6 The new gazebo covers the external staircase and will bond the old and new together.

7 Another internal courtyard, a rich landscape to observe from the living rooms.

8 Inside, the multiple levels create multiple views from within the space.

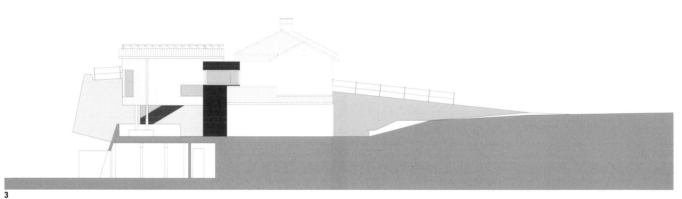

3

4

independent from the old structure, which draws the visitor into a complex of courtyards and inside/outside spaces.

The reconstructed house is arranged roughly as a cruciform, with the new elements running east–west, the old house to the north and a grass slope to the south, described as a 'polite disguise' to shield the new construction from 'nervous parents'. From the western approach a long grass slope rises up to the second-floor level, providing a terrace with views across the park. The east–west forms, culminating in the cantilever, are bold, formed from poured concrete with the shuttering marks visible. The pavilions beyond become smaller and more domestic, the physical equals of the original house. At the centre of the plan is a small courtyard filled with rich red-coloured rocks, a seductive view to gaze upon from within. The new addition to the east is also clad in thin slivers of stone, their form mirroring the wood patterns on the concrete. An external stair runs through the heart of the project, covered by wires which will soon be entwined with wisteria. This gazebo is the 'natural glue' binding old and new.

The external emphasis on changing scale, views and different elements is carried on inside. From the entrance, the view is 'loud and ambitious', almost a 'billboard of status', yet as one proceeds indoors the rooms became more domestic. The public rooms are designed for entertaining, as are the inside/outside spaces, which provide multiple levels and textures for al fresco eating. In contrast, the private rooms are mostly tucked away within the existing house. Only the master bed complex is as bold, jutting out to the east and raised up on pilotis, a public/private pavilion to retreat to and overlook one's dominion.

5

6

7

8

HOME-SCAPE PROJECT

USA

2002

Michael Jantzen

Michael Jantzen is an idiosyncratic architect, providing a very West Coast approach to architecture, one of experimentation and radicalism. His earlier M-house, constructed at the end of the 1990s as a full-scale prototype located north-west of Los Angeles, is half beach hut, half insectoid hive. A self-described conceptual artist whose architectural commissions have rarely extended beyond his immediate family, Jantzen designed the M-house to demonstrate how industrial components can be reappropriated for domestic ends. It was made up of seven cubes, each with opening, folding sides that could create an almost infinite number of façades, and was also scalable, able to expand to fill a suburb, or stack to slot into an urban lot. Home-Scape is a development of this approach – Jantzen describes it as a 'conceptual design study for the development of a new kind of modular manufactured housing system'. Manufactured off-site, it would be transported in the same way as countless thousands of American homes – on the back of a flat-bed truck.

The more structural elements are prefabricated, the more efficient the on-site construction becomes, with such elements as insulation incorporated into the skin. External cladding could be applied after assembly to personalize each individual project. The swooping roofs, which dip down low to the ground, would be clad with a waterproof roofing membrane. Unlike the M-house, the Home-Scape makes extensive use of curves, recalling both the Deco era's obsession with streamlining, and early attempts by post-Modernist architects to break away from the boxy orthodoxy of Modernism. The combination of streamlining and prefabrication echoes earlier ideas on mass-produced Modernist housing, such as Buckminster Fuller's Dymaxion concept.

Around the world, architect-designed prefabricated housing modules are poised to make the leap from dull temporary accommodation to sleek, desirable homes. Modular elements that can be arranged in a distinctly un-boxy manner overcome the principal drawback of the factory-built component – that it must be square in order to fit efficiently on a lorry. However, the real future lies not with relatively specialist low-volume production by joinery companies, but with large-scale factory-based systems modelled on the automobile industry. The aesthetic possibilities of a complex system such as Home-Scape are far ahead of real-world technologies. However, just as the market for automobiles has diversified significantly in the past decade, we can expect prefabrication methods to follow suit.

A more recent project uses off-the-shelf agricultural components as the basis of a new residential architecture. Jantzen believes these could reduce labour costs and address the issue of building waste. He acknowledges that there would need to be a revolution in thinking about domestic architecture before any widespread take-up of the monolithic structural components currently used for barns and storage buildings. Jantzen first used this kind of material in a residential project for his parents more than two decades ago, and the technology has vastly improved since then. Nonetheless, his ideas remain on the fringe.

1 The Home-Scape project is comprised of a series of components that can be used in a variety of different ways.
2 The basic curved elements provide a landscape that is both spatially varied and visually consistent.
3 Jantzen's aesthetic adapts well to numerous uses and scales – this is a recent design for a low-cost prefabricated steel house.

2

3

1

ARTIFICE/MR HOUSE

Pomponne, France

2000

MARIN + TROTTIN / PÉRIPHÉRIQUES

Périphériques is a platform for architec-tural collaboration between the studio of Marin+Trottin and that of Anne-Françoise Jumeau. In recent years, it has reached out into the European architectural community to share ideas and projects with like-minded firms. The Artifice/MR private house in Pomponne was a design study based on theories espoused in their *36 Propositions for a Home* (1997/98), published under the auspices of IN-EX projects.

The design for this single family house was driven by the low budget and narrow, 17-metre (56-foot) long sloping plot. Stepping up in three sections along the site's length, it presents a narrow façade to front and rear gardens. In section view, the house is revealed as a series of four half-storeys. The client was an engineer and DIY enthusiast, with a long-standing dream of living in a metal house, the result of owning a Meccano set in childhood. Thus the entire house is steel-framed, with wood-cement composite panels clipped to the galvanized-steel frame and coloured various shades of green. This form of camouflage, based on a severely pixellated image of the garden, enables the defiantly unnatural materials and shapes to harmonize with surrounding vegetation. Internal walls are lined with plasterboard; the steel trays infilling the frame are left exposed on the underside of the ceilings, with plasterboard cladding on interior walls. The ground-floor slab is poured concrete and staircases and balustrades are stock industrial items. The 140 square metre (1510 square foot) house is entered via a central hallway, with living rooms downhill, sleeping areas uphill.

A recent project for around 30 houses at Rezé, south of Nantes, is the next step in the Périphériques vision for low-cost, innovative housing. The site, Les Jardins de la Pirotterie, is part of a larger, 200-unit scheme constructed on 18 hectares

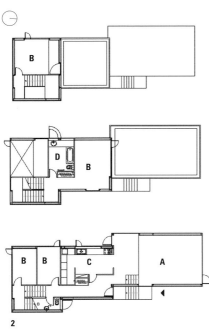

2

3

1. Stepping down a densely wooded site, the Artifice House takes its striking coloration from an abstracted image of the woods.
2. Floor plans: [A] living room, [B] bedroom, [C] kitchen, [D] bathroom.
3. The three elements are offset, allowing views through the long section as well as across.
4. The kitchen ceiling leaves the steel floor trays exposed to complement the house's high-tech feel.

4

5

5, 8 The Icone House at Rezé, designed by Anne
Françoise Jumeau / PÉRIPHÉRIQUES
architectes.

6-7 The Poster House at Rezé, designed by
The Australian Architect.

9 The House Vu by Jacques Moussafir
Architectes.

10 Marin + Trottin's Picnic House: a detail of the
folding window panels on the façade.

6

8

7

9

REZÉ HOUSING

Rezé, France

2005

**MARIN + TROTTIN + JUMEAU /
PÉRIPHÉRIQUES**

(45 acres) of former agricultural land. The architects have arranged their houses in a more organic layout to avoid the repetition of a conventional housing estate, helping them appear naturally integrated with older village houses nearby. The basic concept was to design a building for a housing estate that retained the attractive qualities of one on an open site, perhaps the most pertinent challenge to the twenty-first-century house-builder responding to the cult of consumer individualism.

The architects involved include Marin+Trottin, Paillard and Jumeau, Stalker, Actar and The Australian Architect. Materials are restricted to cheap, unpretentious wood or metal elevations – the Périphériques group concludes that 'we have to upset the production systems that are so economically safe and efficient so that, in time, they too will take part in creating a different town, one that is more poetic and original'. Such projects build on the paradoxes and energy of modern cities, embracing factors that act on current residential architecture: good versus bad, rich versus poor, glamorous versus plain. This collage-like approach is a sort of architectural punk that sets out to challenge conventions established by the planning system and by volume house-builders.

PROJECT CREDITS

the iconic house

introduction

1. High Desert Home
Palm Springs, USA
Kendrick Bangs Kellogg
www.kendrickbangskellogg.com

2. Private House
Hertfordshire, UK
Fraser Brown MacKenna Architects
www.fbmarchitects.com

3. House Nicklaus
Sevenoaks, Kent, UK
m2r Architecture
www.m2r-architecture.com

4. Savage House
USA
Messana O'Rorke Architects
www.messanaororke.com

5. House for a Mogul
Malibu, USA
Jones, Partners: Architecture
www.jonespartners.com

6. Sagaponac House 1
Sagaponac, New York, USA
Field Operations
www.housesatsagaponac.com

7. Grossman Residence
Lanikai, USA/Hawaii
Jim Jennings Architecture
www.jimjenningsarchitecture.com

8. Wheatsheaf House
Victoria, Australia
Jesse Judd Architects
j.judd@a-r-m.com.au

9. House by the Ocean
Stavanger, Norway
Jarmund/Vigsnaes AS Arkitekter
www.jva.no

10. Suitcase House, Commune by the Great Wall of China
Soho China Ltd
www.sohochina.com

DOVER HEIGHTS HOUSE
Sydney, Australia
Architect: Walters and Cohen
Studio 420, Highgate Studios
53–79 Highgate Road
London NW5 1TL
UK
www.waltersandcohen.com
Catherine@waltersandcohen.com
Project team: Cindy Walters, Elaine Henderson
Executive Architect: Collins and Turner
Landscape Design: Barbara Schaffer
Main Contractor: Bellevarde Construction
Landscape: Bellevarde Construction
Engineer: Murtagh Bond
Lighting and Electrical Consultant: Lighting, Art and Science
Client: Private

HAUS NAIRZ
St Georgen, Oberösterreich, Austria
Architect: Gärtner & Neururer ZT GmbH
Stadtplatz 14
4840 Vöcklabruck
Austria
www.gaertner-neururer.at
office@gaertner-neururer.at
Project team: Dr Christian Diridl
Collaborator: Obermayr Holzbau (woodwork)
Client: Adolf U. Gabriele Nairz

ROCHMAN RESIDENCE
Pacific Palisades, California, USA
Architect: Callas Shortridge Architects
3621 Hayden Avenue
Culver City
California 90232
USA
www.callas-shortridge.com
jenn@callas-shortridge.com
Project team: Barbara Callas (principal-in-charge); David Spinelli (project architect); Annie Chu, Michael Matteucci, Damon Caldwell
Landscape Design: Mia Lehrer + Associates (Ester Marqulies – project manager)
Client: Jerry and Doreen Rochman

HOUSE ON THE ALENTEJO COAST
Portugal
Architect: Aires Mateus e Associados
Rua Silva Carvalho 175 r/c
1250-250 Lisbon
Portugal
www.airesmateus.com
m@airesmateus.com;
jps@airesmateus.com
Project team: Manuel Mateus, Francisco Mateus
Client: Private

BELLOWS HOUSE (CASA FUELLE)
Les Preses, Girona, Spain
Architect: RCR Aranda Pigem Vilalta Arquitectes
C/Passeig Blay, 34, 2n pis
17800 Olot (Girona)
Spain
www.rcrarquitectes.es
rcr.arquitectes@coac.es
Project team: M. Tapies, M. Subiràs, A. Saez
Client: Ramon Danés, Lidia Coma

SCHUDEL HOUSE (LIVING SCULPTURE IN THE ALPS)
Feldis, Graubünden, Switzerland
Architect: oos ag open operating system
Schöneggstrasse 5
CH-8004 Zürich
Switzerland
www.oos.com
ad@oos.com
Project team: Severin Boser, Lukas Bosshard, Andreas Derrer, Christoph Kellenberger, Manuel Schudel
Client: Felix and Catherine Schudel

KESSLER HOUSE (HORIZON HOUSE)
Madrid, Spain
Architect: Alberto Morell Sixto
C/Arias Montano 10A
28007 Madrid
Spain
www.albertomorell.com
estudio@albertomorell.com
Project team: Alberto Martínez Carpi,
Jorge Miró Guillem, José Manuel
López-Cela, Daniel Martínez Díaz,
Andrés Toledo Domínguez, Miguel
Angel Hervás (surveyor)
Client: Natalia Gómez del Pozuelo,
Marcos Kessler Grijalvo

DU PLESSIS HOUSE
Paraty, Rio de Janeiro, Brazil
Architect: Marcio Kogan Architect
Al. Tietê
505 São Paulo
Sp Cep 04616-001
Brazil
www.marciokogan.com.br
mk-mk@uol.com.br
Project team: Marcio Kogan
(principal); Diana Radomysler,
Cassia Cavani (project architects);
Bruno Gomes, Oswaldo Pessano,
Paula Moraes, Regiane Leão,
Renata Furlanetto, Samanta
Cafardo, Suzana Glogowski
Landscape Design: Marcelo Faisal
Client: Alberto du Plessis

CASA M AND CASA EQUIS
La Escondida Beach, Cañete, Peru
Architect: Barclay & Crousse
22 rue de la Folie Méricourt
75020 Paris
France
www.barclaycrousse.com
atelier@barclaycrousse.com
Project team: Sandra Barclay,
Edward Barclay, Jean Pierre
Crousse
Site Architect: Edward Barclay
Client: Private

EINFAMILIENHAUS WEISS
Altenmarkt, Salzburg, Austria
Architect: LP Architekten (Lechner
Partner)
Matthäus Lang Gasse 7
5550 Radstadt
Austria
www.lparchitekten.at
lp.architekten@aon.at
Project team: Thomas Lechner,
Alexander Pedevilla (project
architect)
Client: Private

HORTAL HOUSE
Comarruga, El Vendrell, Tarragona,
Spain
Architect: Vicente Guallart
Puig i Xoriguerio
08004 Barcelona
Spain
www.guallart.com
info@guallart.com
Project team: Pilar Gasque, Barbara
Oelbrandt, Cristine Bleichter, Maria
Diaz
Client: Private

HAUS H
Linz, Austria
Architect: Caramel Architekten zt gmbh
– Katherl/Haller/Aspetsberger
Schottenfeldgasse 72/2/3
A-1070 Vienna
Austria
www.caramel.at
kha@caramel.at
Project team: Günter Katherl, Martin
Haller, Ulrich Aspetsberger (project
leader), Clements Kirsch (project
leader), Barbara Schwab
Interior Designer: Friedrich Stiper –
Atelier Tummelplatz
Landscape Architect: Doris Pühringer
Client: Private

HOUSE VM-D
Belgium
Architect and Landscape Design:
Álvaro Siza
Rua do Aleixo 53 – 2
4150-043 Porto
Portugal
www.alvarosiza.com
siza@mail.telepac.pt
Project team: Álvaro Siza, Roberto
Cremascoli (project co-ordinator),
Daniela Antonucci, Maurice
Custers, Andrea Smaniotto, Ueli
Krauss, Christian Kieckens,
Kristofell Boghaert, Karen Van de
Steene, Filip Verbeke
Client: Private

CAMPBELL CLIFFS
Tucson, Arizona, USA
Architect: Line and Space LLC
627 East Speedway
Tucson
Arizona 85705
USA
www.lineandspace.com
Studio627@lineandspace.com
Project team: Les Wallach (project
leader/architect), Robert Clements
(project architect and construction
superintendent), Henry Tom
Collaborators: Elizabeth Rosensteel
Design (furnishings)
Client: Cary and Fern Marmis

BERTHÉ HOUSE (Maison d'Adam
au Paradis)
France
Architect: Moussafir Architectes
Associés
5 rue d'Hauteville
75010 Paris
France
www.moussafir.fr
moussafir.archi@wanadoo.fr
Project team: Jacques Moussafir,
Florent Biais, Christiana Floris,
Lionel Bousquet, Aldric Beckmann,
Gilles Poirée, Rémi Schnebelin,
Laëtitia de Lubac
Client: Private

the city house

introduction

1. Concrete House
London, UK
Azman Architects
www.azmanarchitects.com

2. SUB-'BURB 2025 Concept
Apple Valley, California, USA
Jones, Partners: Architecture
www.jonespartners.com

3. Future House Project
Markland Klaschka Limited
www.marklandklaschka.com

4. Pinch House
London, UK
Foster Lomas
www.fosterlomas.com

5. Hedge House
London, UK
Transient Studio
www.transientstudio.com

6. Nested House v1.03
London, UK
Urban Future Organisation in
collaboration with Michael
Chadwick, Katja Penz (material
research) and Daniel Bosia, Ove
Arup (structures)
www.urbanfuture.org

7. Eco House
Kensington, London, UK
Michaelis Boyd
www.michaelisboyd.com

8. Whatcotts Yard
London, UK
Annalie Riches, Silvia Ullmayer and
Barti Garibaldo

9. Gae House
Tokyo, Japan
Atelier Bow-Wow
www.bow-wow.jp

10. Seatrain
Los Angeles, USA
Office of Mobile Design
www.designmobile.com

11. Donnybrook Quarter
London, UK
Peter Barber Architects
www.peterbarberarchitects.com

12. Anderson House
London, UK
Jamie Fobert Architects
www.jamiefobertarchitects.com

PRIVATE HOUSE IN SUBURB
Kuldtiiva 12, Tallinn, Estonia
Architect: 3+1 Architects
Raua 12-1
Tallinn 10124
Estonia
www.threeplusone.ee
mail@threeplusone.ee
Project team: Markus Kaasik, Andres
Ojari, Ilmar Valdur with Kalle
Komissarov, Merje Müürisepp,
Indrek Tiigi
Client: Maike and Rein Iida

CASA ON THE CAMPO DEL PRÍNCIPE
Granada, Spain
Architect: Ramón Fernández-Alonso
Borrajo
Dirección Caidero 14
19009 Granada
Spain
f.alonso@coagranada.org
Collaborators: Cuadrado Saenz
(architect), José Miguel Vazquez
(structural engineer/architectural
supervisor)
Client: Familia Ruiz-Jiménez

HOUSE FOR TWO ARTISTS
Clerkenwell, London, UK
Architect: Tony Fretton Architects
49–59 Old Street
London EC1V 9XH
UK
www.tonyfretton.co.uk
cc@tonyfretton.co.uk
Project team: Tony Fretton, Jim
McKinney, David Owen, Matt
Barton, Simon Jones, Karin Hepp
Interiors: Tony Fretton Architects;
Tim Wright and Jo Pettiward
Client: Tim Wright and Jo Pettiward

KLEIN HOUSE
Inageku, Chiba, Japan
Architect: Norisada Maeda Atelier
Glass House 1F
1-9-5 Izumi-honcyo
Komae-shi
Tokyo 201-0003
Japan
www5a.biglobe.ne.jp
miyamoto.shinqgiga.ocn.ne.jp
Project team: Yoshichka Takagi,
Noriko Tsuno, Mitsunobu
Yamagishi
Client: Mr and Mrs Kimura

HOUSE ON BACON STREET
Bethnal Green, London, UK
Architect: William Russell, Pentagram
Design
11 Needham Road
London W11 2RP
UK
www.pentagram.co.uk
adams@pentagram.co.uk
Project team: William Russell; Jon
Mangham, Zeno Deitrich
(assistants); Sheila Muiry (project
manager)
Client: Private residence for William
Russell

**MUJI + INFILL KINOIE HOUSE,
JAPAN**
Architect: Kazuhiko + Namba +
KAI – Workshop for Ryohin Keikaku
Co. Ltd (Muji), Japan
4-26-3 Higashi-Ikebukuro
Toshima-ku
Tokyo 170-8424
Japan
www.muji.net/infill
sugiyama@muji.net
Client: Muji

STEALTH HOUSE

Denmark Hill, London, UK
Architect: Robert Dye Associates
Unit a2, Linton House
39–51 Highgate Road
London NW5 1RS
UK
www.robertdye.com
info@robertdye.com
Project team: Robert Dye, Jason
Coleman, Nico Stassano
Collaborators: Geoff Powell (interior
furniture), Greig-Ling (consulting
engineer on the timber construction)
Client/Self-builder: Greig-Ling

HAUS KARG

Augsburg, Haunstetten, Germany
Architect: Regina Schineis Architektin
bda
Hochfeldstrasse 2
86159 Augsburg
Germany
www.schineis.com
buero@schineis.com
Project team: Regina Schineis, Dina
Hilliges (project architect)
Client: T. and B. Karg

NATURAL WEDGE

Tokyo, Japan
Architect: Masaki Endoh and Masahiro
Ikeda – Endoh Design House (EDH)
and MIAS
2-13-8 Honnmachi
Shibuya-ku
Tokyo 151-0071
Japan
wwww.edh-web.com
edh-endoh-mvi@biglobe.ne.jp
Project team: Masaki Endoh, Rio
Tomita, Kenji Nawa, Hirofumi Ohno
Client: Y.H.

NATURAL ELLIPSE

Tokyo, Japan
Architect: Endoh Design House (EDH) +
MIAS
2-13-8 Honnmachi
Shibuya-ku
Tokyo 151-0071
Japan
wwww.edh-web.com
edh-endoh-mvi@biglobe.ne.jp
Project team: Masaki Endoh,
Masahiro Ikeda
Client: K.H. and S.H.

the practical house

introduction

1. Cedar House

North Elmham, Norfolk, UK
Hudson Architects
www.hudsonarchitects.co.uk

2. House in Cambridge

Massachusetts, USA
Uni-Architecture: Chaewon Kim
www.uni-arch.com

3. House and Studio Lang-Kröll

Gleissenberg, Germany
Florian Nagler Architekten
www.nagler-architekten.de

4. Sparrow House

Lewes, UK
BBM Architects
www.bbm-architects.co.uk

5. RuralZed

Devon, UK
Bill Dunster Architects
www.zedfactory.com

6. Flexi-Log System

Stuart Harris-Hancock
technoworlock@yahoo.com

7. The Paper House Concept

Adriano Pupilli
www.thepaperhouse.net

8. Optima Homes Concept

Cartwright Pickard
www.optimahomes.co.uk

9. modular2house

Studio 804, University of Kansas
School of Architecture and Urban
Design
www.studio804.com

10. Pad Modular Homes

Pad – Michael Wallis
www.padlife.co.uk

11. Villa Nesselande, Rotterdam

The Netherlands
Hopman Architecten
www.hopmanarchitecten.nl

12. House in Germany

John Pawson Architects
www.johnpawson.co.uk

KUNGSHATT SUMMER HOUSE

Lake Mälaren, Sweden
Architects: Peter Hesselgren and
Gunvor Larsson
Åsögatan 119
S-116 24 Stockholm
Sweden
www.ssark.se
gunvor.larsson@telia.com
Project team: Peter Hesselgren,
Gunvor Larsson with Joel
Hesselgren
Client: Peter Hesselgren, Gunvor
Larsson

YALE SCHOOL OF ARCHITECTURE 2004
BUILDING PROJECT

Architect: Yale School of Architecture
Building Project
180 York Street
New Haven
Connecticut 06511
USA
www.architecture.yale.edu
lkbrouard@snet.net
Client: Neighborhood Housing
Services

HOUSE AT CASTETNER

Pyrénées-Atlantiques, France
Architect: L'Atelier Provisoire
59 rue de la Rousselle
33000 Bordeaux
France
atelierprovisoire@free.fr
Project team: Aline Rodrigues
Lefore, Laurent Vilette, Hélène
Soubiron, Pascale de Tourdonnet,
Rafael Santamairia
Collaborator: Agence Coudeneau
Client: Private

MARSH VIEW HOUSE
Norfolk, UK
Architect: Lynch Architects
147a Hoxton Street
London N1 6OG
UK
www.lyncharchitects.co.uk
lyncharchitects@btopenworld.com
Project team: Patrick Lynch, Jacques
Dahan, Naomi Shaw
Client: Alison Mitchell

HOUSE IN AGGSTALL
Freising, Upper Bavaria, Germany
Architect: Hild und K Architekten
Nikolaistrasse 2
80802 Munich
Germany
www.hildundk.de
architekten@hildundk.de
Project team: Andreas Hild, Dionys
Ottl (partners in charge); Dirk Bayer,
Birgit Breu, Claudia von Hessert,
Thomas Thalhofer, Andreas Kretzer,
Jens Schelling
Client: Barbara Gross, Dr Berthold
Schwarz

THE BOX HOUSE
New South Wales, Australia
Architect: Neeson Murcutt Architects
Level 5
71 York Street
Sydney NSW 2000
Australia
nmurcutt@iprimus.com.au
Project team: Nick Murcutt, Rachel
Neeson, Temera Ripamonti
Collaborators: Colin Jack (builder),
Marsh and Associates (engineers)
Client: Martin Halstead, Liz Charles

HOUSE IN WANDLITZ
Berlin, Germany
Architect: Heide von Beckerath Alberts
Architekten
Kürfürstendamm 173
10707 Berlin
Germany
www.hyp95.de
mail@hyp95.de
Project team: Tim Heide, Verena von
Beckerath, Andrew Alberts
Client: Private

MAISON DEJARDIN-HENDRICÉ
Comblain-au-Pont, Belgium
Architect: Atelier d'Architecture Pierre
Hebbelinck S.A.
Rue Fond Pirette, 43
B-4000 Liège
Belgium
www.pierrehebbelinck.net
Pierre.hebbelinck@skynet.be
Client: André Dejardin, Magali
Hendricé

BLUE HOUSE
London, UK
Architects: FAT
116–20 Golden Lane
London EC1Y OTF
UK
www.fat.co.uk
fat@fat.co.uk
Project team: Sean Griffiths, Sam
Jacob, Charles Holland, Dmitrij
Kudin, Laura Cramwinkel, Mie
Olise, Sacha Leong, Deborah Reis
Client: Lynn Kinnear

SUMMER HOUSE
Åland, Finland
Architect: Todd Saunders and Tommie
Wilhelmsen
Nygårdsgaten 2a
5015 Bergen
Norway
www.saunders-wilhelmsen.no
post@saunders-wilhelmsen.no
Project team: Todd Saunders,
Tommie Wilhelmsen

MUKAROV HOUSE
Prague, Czech Republic
Architect: Ivan Kroupa Architects
Osadni 46
17000 Prague 7
Czech Republic
www.ivankroupa.cz
ivankroupa@ivankroupa.cz
Project team: Ivan Kroupa, Radka
Kurcíková (collaborator)

COURTYARD HOUSES
Matosinhos, Portugal
Architect: Souto Moura Arquitectos
Lda
Rua de Aleixo, 53 – 1oA
4150-043 Porto
Portugal
souto.moura@mail.telepac.pt
Project team: Silvia Alves, Manuela
Lara, Filipe Pinto da Cruz, Teresa
Gonçalves, Laura Peretti
Client: Miguel Pereira Leite and
others

MAISON MALICE
Brussels, Belgium
Architect: Jean Leclercq
81 avenue Paul Deschanel
B-1030 Brussels
Belgium
www.delicesarchitectes.com
info@delicesarchitectes.com
Project team: Cédric Callens, Benoit
Frisson, Jean Leclercq, Stephane
Moetwil

DESIGN>BUILD>TEXAS
Johnson City, Texas, USA
Architect: University of Texas at Austin,
School of Architecture
University of Texas at Austin
Goldsmith Hall 2.310
Austin, Texas 78712
USA
www.ar.utexas.edu
harpman@mail.utexas.edu
Associate Dean for Undergraduate
Programs: Louise Harpman
Professor: Harwell Hamilton Harris

HOUSE AND STUDIO

Münsterland, Germany
Architect: Léon Wohlhage Wernik
Gessellschaft von Architekten mbH
Leibnizstrasse 65
Metahaus
10629 Berlin
Germany
www.leonwohlhagewernik.de
post@leonwohlhagewernik.de
Project team: Prof. Hilde Léon,
Lonrad Wohlhage, Siegfried Wernik
(partners in charge); Peter Deluse,
Ulrich Vetter, Werner Mayer-Biela,
Bettina Zalenga
Landscape Design:
S.A.L. Planungsgruppe

VILLA HOOFDDORP

Floriande, Netherlands
Architect: Paul Verhey Architecten
M. van B. Bastiaansestraat 15
1054 RS Amsterdam
Netherlands
www.verheyarchitecten.nl
info@verheyarchitecten.nl
Project team: Paul Verhey (project
architect)
Collaborators: Martijn Anhalt, Paulus
Egers (interior design)
Client: Hans van der Aar

BRICK LEAF HOUSE

Hampstead, London, UK
Architects: Woolf Architects
27 Swinton Street
London WC1X 9NW
UK
www.contemporary-
architecture.com
woolf.architects@virgin.net
Project team: Jonathan Woolf,
Christopher Snow, Medine Altiok,
Stuart Cughlin, Thomas Goodey,
Harvey Langston-Jones, Laurent
Pereira, Susan Russell, Andy
Wakefield
Landscape Design: Schoenaich Rees
Associates

CAMPEGGIO NEL BOSCO

Collalto Sabino, Italy
Architect: T Studio/Guendalina Salimei
Architetto
Guendalina Salimei
Piazza A. Mancini, 4
00196 Roma
Italy
t.studio@tiscalinet.it
Project team: Marco Bottoni,
Francesca Contuzzi (collaborators);
Bruno Giuseppini, Giuditta Vicari
(consultants); Dino Giuseppini
(director of work)
Client: Comune di Collalto Sabino

BLACK HOUSE

Cambridgeshire, UK
Architects: Meredith Bowles, Mole
Architects
The Black House
Kingdon Avenue
Prickwillow CB7 4UL
UK
www.molearchitects.co.uk
studio@molearchitects.co.uk
Project team: Meredith Bowles,
Kirsten Hagart
Collaborators: JJO Associates
(building engineers); Martyn
Gamble (energy consultants)
Client: Mole Architects

the future house

introduction

1. Futureshack
Sean Godsell Architects
www.seangodsell.com

2. Modern Modular
Resolution: 4 Architecture
www.re4a.com

3. 4 × 8 House
London, UK
Project Orange Architects
www.projectorange.com

4. Q Series Home
Canada
Royal Homes
www.royalhomes.com

5. Prefabricated Housing
Rollalong Ltd
www.rollalong.co.uk

6. Quik-House
Kalkin & Co
www.architectureandhygiene.com

7. Container City
London, UK
Eric Reynolds/Nicholas Lacey
www.containercity.com

8. LV Home
Rocio Romero Design
www.rocioromero.com

9. Style House – Pure/Fun/Pop
Hackenbroich Architeken
www.hackenbroich.com

10. Glidehouse
Menlo Park, California, and
Chelon, Washington, USA
Michelle Kaufmann Designs
www.glidehouse.com

PALM SPRINGS MODULAR HOUSE

Slovenia
Architect: Maechtig Vrhunc Arhitekti
Slovenska 55a
SI-1000 Ljubljana
Slovenia
www.mvarch.com
mva@mvarch.com
Client/Manufacturer: Riko Hise d.o.o.

M7 PROTOTYPE

Tunquèn, Chile
Architect: UR01.ORG cooperative
José Ramón Guitiérrez 282 piso 2
832-0162 Santiago
Chile
www.uro1.org
alejandro@uro1.org
Project team: Fernando Portal,
Nicholás Rebolledo, Gabriel
Rudolphy, Alejandro Soffia, Arturo
Torre
Construction Project team: Jaime
Aravena, Familia Montoya, Me
José Varas, Rodrigo Gijón, Jaime
Lorca, Alejandro Soffia Vial, Daniel
Soffia Vega, LuLa, Rodrigo Del
Castillo, Jaime Pascual, 'Rambo'
Collaborators: José Vega (plywood
components); Segundo Rodriguez
(fibreglass)
Client: Jaime Aravena

TWENTY PROPOSITIONS FOR SUBURBAN LIVING

Raleigh, North Carolina, USA
Architect: Borden Partnership LLP
2312 Bedford Avenue
Raleigh
North Carolina 27607
USA
www.bordenpartnership.com
gail_borden@ncsu.edu
Project team: Gail Peter Borden,
Brooke Taylor Borden

PARASITE PARADISE

Leidsche Rijn, Utrecht, Netherlands
Organizer: Bureau Beyond
Gemeente Utrecht
Postbus 8613 RP Utrecht
030-2867100
Netherlands
www.beyondutrecht.nl
bureaubeyond@utrecht.nl
List of collaborating artists/architects:
Miele Ruimtestation (2012
Architecten); Mobile Linear City
(Vito Acconci); Mobiele Keuken
(Maximee Ansiau); Pioniersset
(Atelier van Lieshout); Mini Capsule
Side Entrance – 6 units (Atelier van
Lieshout); Mobile (André van
Bergen); Nomads in Residence
(Bik van der Pol – Korteknie
Stuhlmacher Architecten); Mobile
Porch (Böhm/Saffer/Lang); Markies
(Eduard Böhtlingk); Camping Falt
(Kevin van Braak); Urban Design
Parasite Paradise (Luc Deleu);
Zuzatrzraum and Zuzatzraum –
Enghien Les Bain (Exilhäuser
Architekten); Light Building (Atelier
Kempe Thill Architects and
Planners); Hotelit (Vadim Fishkin en
Yuri Leiderman); Room With a View
(HAP); Mobile Greenhouse (Ed
Joosting Bunk/Plan de Campagne);
Agora Phobia – Digitalis (Karen
Lancel); Boerenwereldkeuken
Restaurant (Maurer United
Architects); Mobile Unit Shed
(Daniel Milohnic en Dirk Paschke
Resonatorcoop); Viva el Monopatin
(Maurer United Architects);
ParaSITE (Kas Oosterhuis, Ilona
Lénárd, Menno Rubbens: Attila
Foundation); Tsantiri-Hall (Stefanos
Tsivopoulos); Bar Reketa (Inge
Roseboom, Mark Weemen);
Design for 'tractorfabriek' (Rob
Vrijen); Dodenbivak (Dré
Wapenaar); Lichtspeilhuas
(Wolfgang Winter en Berthold
Hörbelt)
Client: Municipality of Utrecht

UP!HOUSE

USA
Architect: Craig Konyk Architecture
61 Pearl Street No.509
Brooklyn
New York 11201-8339
USA
www.konyk.net
www.up-house.com
konyk@konyk.net
Project team: Craig Konyk

HOUSE D

Velenje, Slovenia
Architect: Sadar Vuga Arhitekti
Cankarjevo Nabrezje 11/III
1000 Ljubljana
Slovenia
www.sadarvuga.com
biro@sadarvuga.com
Project team: Jurij Sadar, Boštjan
Vuga, Miha Pešec, Adrian Petrucelli
Structural Engineer: Jani Ramsak
Service Engineers: KPV, PE
Energetika – Marjan Pecovnik
(Mechanical), Esotech – Robert
Lindic (Electrical)
Lighting: Arcadia
Client: Private

ELDORADO CANYON RESIDENCE

Boulder County, Colorado, USA
Architects: Building Studio
431 South Main Street
Second Floor
Memphis
Tennessee 38103
USA
www.buildingstudio.net
ccocker@buildingstudio.net
Project team: Coleman Coker,
Jonathan Tate, Carl Batton Kennon,
Christopher Schmidt, Brad Smith
Landscape Architect: The Landscape
Studio
Client: Private

LIVING ROOM HOUSE
Gelnhausen, Germany
Architects: Seifert and Stöckmann
Architekten
Mörfelder Landstrasse 72
D-60598 Frankfurt am Main
Germany
www.formalhaut.de
seifer.stoeckmann@formalhaut.de
Project team: Gabriela Seifert, Götz
Stöckmann
Collaborators: Ludger Gerdes
(painting), Ottmar Hörl
(photography), Georg Hüter
(sculpture), Thomas Kling (lyrics),
Wolfgang Luy (sculpture), Scott
Murff (installation), Catherine
Spellman (installation), Charly
Steiger (light), Achim Wollscheid
(noise)
Client: seifert.stöckmann

FISHERMAN'S HOUSE
Asti, Piedmont, Italy
Architect: Studio Elastico
Corso Duca degli Abruzzi 14
Torino
Italy
www.studioeleastico.com
elastico@studioeleastico.com
Project team: Stefano Pujatii (project
leader), Simone Carena, Alberto del
Maschio, Davide Musmeci, Cristina
Negri, Luca Macrì, Giovanni Tironi,
Manuela Luis y Garcia, Ester
Musso, Alex Morassut, Francisco
Del Gado
Collaborators: Cesario Carena, Ditta
Interni (interior)
Client: Private

HOME-SCAPE PROJECT
USA
Architect: Michael Jantzen
27800 McBean Parkway, Suite 319
Valencia
California 91354
USA
www.humanshelter.org
mjantzen@yahoo.com

ARTIFICE/MR HOUSE
Pomponne, France
Architect: Périphériques: Marin +
Trottin
8 rue Montcalm
75018 Paris
France
www.peripheriques-
architectes.com
mt_arch@club-internet.fr
Project team: Emmanuelle Marin-
Trottin, David Trottin, Rafael Falcon,
Daniel Graignic
Client: Martin/Rodriguez

REZÉ HOUSING
France
Architect: Périphériques: Marin +
Trottin + Jumeau
8 rue Montcalm
75018 Paris
France
www.peripheriques-
architectes.com
mt_arch@club-internet.fr
Project team: Emmanuelle Marin-
Trottin, David Trottin, Rafael Falcon,
Daniel Graignic

PICTURE CREDITS

Fernando Alda (100–3), Louis Ferreura Alves (172–4), Courtesy the architects (166–7), Satoshi Asakawa (28), Paul Bardagjy (181–3), Susan Barr (117 bottom, 146 right, 147), Peter Bennetts (27 middle), Hélène Binet (23 top, 104–5, 193–5), Brett Boardman (152–5), Jeen Boetzel (133 bottom), Courtesy Michaelis Boyd (90 bottom left), Laurent Brandjas (177–9), Adrian Briscoe/granddesignmagazine.com (13), Earl Carter (202), Leon Chew (16 third down, 18), Keith Collie (86), Andrés Cortinez and Maria José Arce (214, 215 top), Gilles Coulon, Tendance Floue (83–5), J.P. Crousse (60–3), André Dejardin (161 bottom), Peter de Ru (137–9), John Donat (198–201), Thomas Drexl (119), Courtesy Robert Dye Associates (114–17 top), Courtesy Foster Lomas (89 bottom left), Christian Gahl (156–9), Jean-Christophe Garcia (140, 142–5), Dennis Gilbert/VIEW (94), Richard Glover/VIEW (30–3), Kaido Haagen (96, 99 top and middle), Roland Halbe/artur (74–7), Daniel Hannisy (93 top right), Michael Heindrich (150–1), Sarah Hewson (209 top), Hertha Hurnais (72–3), Werner Huthmacher (134), Hypertecture (24 top), Courtesy IKEA Press Department (19 second down), Courtesy Jaguar Cars (14), Courtesy Jarmund/Vigsnaes AS Arkitekter (27 bottom), Jim Jennings Architecture (27 top), Courtesy Jones, Partners (24 middle, 89 top), Courtesy Kalkin & Company (206 bottom), Ralph Kamena (220–1), Michelle Kaufmann Designs (210), Chaewon Kim (129 top), Nikolaus Korab (34–7), Ivan Kroupa (168, 169 bottom, 170–1), Courtesy Lazor Office (17 top), Quirin Leppert (228–31), Courtesy Levittown Public Library (10), Courtesy m2r-architecture (23 bottom), Raf Makda/VIEW (165 top), Daniel Malhão – DMF Fotografia (2–3, 43–5), Arne Maasik (98, 99 bottom), Shinji Miyamoto (106–7), Courtesy Optima Homes (130 bottom right), K. O'Sullivan (90 bottom right), Courtesy Muji (112–13), Oscar Paisley (164 bottom, 165 bottom), Arnaldo Pappalardo (8, 57–9), Courtesy Pattern (12 bottom), Courtesy Périphériques (239–41), Matteo Piazza (169 top), Pino Dell'Aquila (232–5), Marie-Françoise Plissart (160–1 top), Eugeni Pons (46–7), Ramon Pratt (69–71), Adriano Pupili (130 bottom left), Robert Reck (78–81), Ed Reeve (108–111), Christian Richters (184–7), Simone Rosenberg (29 middle), Courtesy Royal Homes (205 bottom), Hiro Sakaguchi (120–5), Leigh Simpson (129 bottom), Rupert Steiner (64–7), Courtesy Studio 804 (133 top), Edmund Sumner/VIEW (93 top left), Hisao Suzuki (52–4), Courtesy T Studio (196–7), Steve Townsend – zzzone imaging & photography (126), Courtesy Toyota Housing Corporation (19 bottom), Courtesy Transient/Jonathan Pile (89 bottom right), Courtesy Ushida Findlay (15), Morley von Sternberg (93 bottom, 162), Courtesy Michael Wallis (133 middle), architekturbild/Dominique Marc Wehrli (48–51), Alan Weintraub/ARCAID (20), Michael Weschler (16 second down, 38–41), Luke White (146 left, 148), Henry Yamamoto (226), Juan Alfonso Zapata (215 bottom), Kim Zwarts (188–91).

INDEX

Page numbers in *italics* refer to picture captions

ACKNOWLEDGEMENTS

My sincere thanks to all the architects and designers who supplied images and information for this book, as well as to Claire Curtice and Laura Iloniemi. I'm also eternally grateful to the team at Laurence King, including Philip Cooper, Kirsty Seymour-Ure, John Jervis, Adam Hooper and especially Jennifer Hudson for her tireless work with the often obscure images.

Thank you most of all to Alex and Toby.